CONTENTS

Preface		5
1	Starting Out	7
2	Birth	16
3	Growing Up	25
4	Sex	41
5	Marriage	55
6	The Family	68
7	Old Age	74
8	Death . . . and Beyond?	83

PREFACE

From the Cradle to the Grave is designed to provide a year's coursework for fourth or fifth form non-examination classes. Some of the material would also be useful for PSE courses and for GCSE RE. The course is based on a study of the life cycle, moving from sociological and psychological issues to moral and existential ones, and overtly religious material is then introduced. The religious content is thus 'life-grounded' and therefore more relevant.

The religious approach is multi-faith, drawing generally on Hinduism, Sikhism, Judaism, Christianity and Islam. Scriptural references are given from the last three faiths listed because of accessibility. The reason for a multi-faith approach is that many pupils will share very different ethical presuppositions and very different life-stances from their classmates. Christian ethics and beliefs are also adequately covered since Christianity has played a significant role in the formation of British society and moral thinking.

The various rites of passage are presented in the form of summary picture-strips at the end of some chapters, and should provide a basic and clear guide both for the less able and the more able pupil. Each page usually presents a new aspect of a topic that could be studied in a lesson. The exercises cover a variety of skills — creative expression, discussion, comprehension and role-play.

K. O'D.

1 STARTING OUT

Our world

The Earth is roughly 4,500 million years old, and it is one of nine planets that orbit the sun. Our Solar System is in the Milky Way Galaxy, a cluster of about 100,000 million stars. There are nearly 100 million galaxies that we know of; the furthest of these is about 10,000 million light-years away, and it can only be seen as a faint glow by our most powerful telescopes. (Light travels 9.6 million million kilometres in a year, hence the term 'light-year'.) How did this vast universe begin?

Scientists have discovered two things that help them to work out an answer:

1. The galaxies are moving apart from each other at vast speeds; the faster the further away from us they are.
2. There is a background radiation all through the universe, like a cosmic humming.

Taking these two facts into consideration, most scientists think that the universe was started by a huge explosion at the dawn of time, a 'big bang'. This scattered gases and chemicals and molecules through space, and these eventually formed the stars and planets. Hence, the galaxies are moving apart, still under the impact of the Big Bang, and the background radiation is a leftover from it.

Some scientists reject the Big Bang theory, but most accept it as the most likely explanation for the origin of the universe. Yet no one can say what came before the Big Bang. Some think there might have been a very, very small particle of matter that was infinitely dense, or heavy, and when it became too dense it exploded.

Science-fiction writers like to play around with the idea of a 'concertina universe', thinking that it is forever expanding and collapsing in on itself again. This seems unlikely, as there is no clear limit to how far the galaxies can expand – they could just go on for ever. Also, some scientists think that there would be far more heat in the universe if it had exploded in and out over and over again.

Other scientists think that the universe just happened, out of nothing. There would have been no immensely small particle of matter, everything would just have exploded into existence and formed slowly, including space and time itself.

We do not know how far the universe extends. Is there an end to it, or does it go on for ever? Are there other, different universes out there somewhere?

Our earliest ancestors were living about two to three million years ago. Fossil bones have been found in Kenya that show the existence of a human-like creature with a brain about two-thirds the size of ours. He could sharpen stones to make simple tools, and thus he has been nicknamed *homo habilis*, the 'handyman'! Other fossil bones from later times show that brain size and speech ability was becoming more advanced, until we arrived on the scene about 50,000 years ago. (*Homo sapiens sapiens* means 'wise man'.)

Once we have taken all these facts about our world and the evolution of humankind into account, some important questions remain: 'Are human beings special in any way, or will a more advanced species take over the world in the future?' Humankind seems to be the dominant species at the moment. This is because our

Skull of *homo habilis* found by Dr Richard Leaky in 1972 at Lake Turkana

Would these work in a different way, with different laws of physics? If you dropped something there, would it fly up into the air rather than dropping to the ground? Who knows? Still, it is interesting to think about such things, difficult though they might be! It stretches our imagination and makes us more aware of the mysteries of this huge universe that we live in.

We do not know how many planets support life. Maybe many out of the billions in the universe do, but it seems likely that the only one to do so in our Solar System is our own, the planet Earth. Life developed here because certain chemicals came together in the right combination (carbon dioxide, ammonia and hydrogen cyanide). Life seems to have developed over millions of years, from simple one-celled creatures about 600 million years ago to the wide variety of species that we have today, including ourselves, *homo sapiens sapiens*. The more intelligent animals developed complicated electrical nervous systems as their brains increased in size. That is why we are friendlier to horses, dogs and cats than we are to ants, for example. We have more in common.

brains have evolved to the point where we can reason things out. We can think for ourselves, and we can make tools and instruments that allow us to change our surroundings. When these two things are put together, the reason and the hands, then we can investigate our world and we can change it – for the better or for the worse! (This is not to say that other animals have no intelligence. Many obviously do – watch dogs and cats in action, for example. A creature like the dolphin shows deep friendship and feeling for other creatures, and their high-pitched sounds are a form of language. They might even be telepathic, reading each other's minds! The point is that human intelligence seems to be more advanced in other ways.)

Some people think that human beings are the dominant species by luck and accident; it just happened that our species changed and adapted in the best way and we climbed to the top of the ladder. Others think that humans were intended by God to be the most responsible creature on Earth. God guided our evolution, or we just evolved by chance; neither idea can be proved. What do you think?

Whatever we believe, humans have a tremendous responsibility. We have power over the Earth – we can develop and help it, or we can damage it. We can cure diseases and help crops to grow better, or we can pollute rivers and kill off forests, and even destroy all life with our nuclear weapons.

Another question is: 'Why is the universe here at all? What are we all doing here?' Scientists do not try to work out what the point of it all is, they just try to find out *how* it works, *how* it all fits together. The universe might have started with the Big Bang, but whatever for? Did it all happen by chance, or was something planning it? Scientists are concerned with mechanisms, how things fit together, not with personal things like meanings.

Some people look at life and they think: 'It just happened. Live your life, make the best of it that you can, and that's all there is to it! There's no reason for being here.' If that is true, then you have to make up your own meanings – life is special and is to be lived, even if it just happened by accident. It is wrong to think that nothing matters and people do not matter, even if you do not think there is any meaning to the universe. Choose Life! Respect Life!

Many other people think that some power or force planned the universe and has been guiding it. This power or force is called God. Ancient people made up many stories to try to imagine how God might have made the world. Some might seem crude and childish to us today, such as this one from Babylon:

Everything was a watery chaos at first. The god Marduk challenged the chaos, which was pictured as a goddess or dragon called Tiamat. Marduk slew Tiamat and carved up her body. From this, Marduk made the world.

You might laugh at this at first, but treat it as a parable, or a picture-story. Order and life developed out of chaos only because of a guiding intelligence. Ancient people did not think the world had come about by chance. Note that modern scientists also think that everything was chaotic at the start of the universe, when the Big Bang happened.

A more familiar story is from the Bible, from the Book of Genesis, chapter one. This was written down by the Jews, about 2,500 years ago, based on a story that had been handed down by word of mouth for generations.

The idea of the world being made in six days sounds silly to us, but in that story is again the idea of order and life coming out of chaos by the power of a guiding intelligence. Few people who believe in God think that God made the world in six days; they think God was at work over millions of years and is still at work today.

Some people think that these old stories were made up because people did not know about science then, and so now we can forget about them. If you do forget about them, however, perhaps you are ignoring their insights. They are more concerned with meanings than mechanisms – they are an idea of what the world is all about, and not just an attempt to work out how it has come about. Some today think the universe happened by chance, some think God planned it. There is no proof either way; it is an open question, and there are intelligent people who hold either view. It is something to think about as you go through life.

In the beginning, when God created the universe, the earth was formless and chaotic. Raging waters covered everything, and there was darkness everywhere. The power of God moved over the waters, and God commanded light to shine in the darkness. God continued to work and continued to send out his word which created all types of life. After creating humans, God rested on the seventh day.

Rites of passage

You are alive, and you are on a journey. You are taking part in the journey of life, from birth right through to death. There are special times and important milestones in life's journey such as birth, reaching maturity and adulthood, getting married, raising a family, retiring from work and growing old and, finally, dying. These milestones are like markers along the road of life, and different cultures have customs and rituals to help us to understand the importance of each of these milestones and to help us to get through them and move on. These customs and rituals, these special actions and beliefs, are called 'rites of passage'. These help us to pass from one stage of life into another.

Religions have their own 'rites of passage' as do non-religious groups and people. Religions try to give people the idea that God is going along life's journey with them, and can guide them along. Yet, even if some people are unsure about the existence of God, they still need guidance. They still need to make sense of the life they are living. We all need to feel that our lives are going somewhere and are worth living. We grow confused, angry, frustrated and even mentally ill if we cannot see any purpose in our lives. Rites of passage help to give us guidance and some direction along life's path.

How do I decide what to do?

As we grow up, we are faced with many choices, such as:

'What job can I get when I leave school?'

'What type of person do I want to marry, if I marry at all?'

'What do I do with my money?'

'What do I want out of life?'

We are also faced with many *moral* choices, where we have to decide what we think is right and wrong. Human beings are able to make choices like that; we do not just live by instinct, doing what our feelings tell us. We have to think of other people around us too. If we just pleased ourselves all the time, then other people would suffer because of our selfishness.

People have different ways of working out what they think is right and wrong. Here are some of the ways:

1. **'It's all right so long as you get away with it!'**

   In other words, be as selfish as you like so long as you avoid trouble. So, stealing is OK so long as you don't get caught.

2. **'Do this or else!'**

   People might do something because they are afraid of being punished – perhaps by parents, teachers, the Law or even God. (The 'you go to heaven if you're good, hell if you're bad' idea.)

3. **'You scratch my back, and I'll scratch yours!'**

   You do someone else a good turn so long as they will do you one back.

4. **'It is written!'**

   You do something because the Law says that it is OK, or because your religion says it is. You don't think about it for yourself, you obey what the authorities say.

5. **'My mates say it's OK!'**

   You go along with your group of friends. You do what is acceptable to them. You don't want to feel left out.

6. **'Do it because it's right!'**

   Think about it yourself, and do what seems best to you. Do what is good for its own sake, not for what you get out of it, or for what people think of you.

Reason 6 is the most mature reason for taking a course of action. All the others are either selfish ('what can I get out of it'), or they are thoughtless ('go along with the crowd', 'obey authority'). It is the hardest one to follow, though. It makes you think, and to think properly you have to be ready to learn new ideas.

To work out your own opinions on things, you need to be able to talk to other people and to listen to what they have to say. You need to find out certain facts and figures about an issue. For example, if your friends are telling you that it does you no harm to smoke, then find out what the medical facts are; don't just take their word for it! Then make up your own mind.

There is one basic rule to test whether something is right or wrong – will it hurt someone else? You might want some money for new clothes, but if you steal it, then someone else will lose out and be hurt. A car-driver might want to ignore a red light, but he might knock someone down or cause a crash if he does.

You might also want to consider whether or not an action will hurt yourself. Smoking might damage your health, for example, or too much alcohol might get you into a fight or into a road accident.

A religious person would also add, 'Will my actions be hurtful to God?'

Religions have many lists of 'rights and wrongs' to guide their followers. These moral guidelines are sometimes written out in lists and these form moral codes. The Ten Commandments in the Jewish and Christian traditions are a good example. Muslims are careful to try to follow the moral instructions given in various passages of their holy book, the Qur'an, and other religions have their codes and scriptures too. Some religious people think that the moral codes in their scriptures were inspired by God; they are God's will and must never be questioned. This idea sees the writers of the codes as 'God's secretaries', people who take down God's words.

Some other religious people do not think this. They take their scriptures and their codes as the words of holy people who were trying to find out God's will.

However, they might have made some mistakes, or they wrote more for the people of their own day than ours. These religious people use their codes more as guidelines rather than as rules, and they will only follow them if they think they are good and the best thing to do.

All religions agree that what God wants above all else is for people to live in peace and to love one another. Muslims, for example, believe that they should try to be compassionate and merciful, just as God is. Then again, Jesus summed up the Law of Moses by saying that it all came down to loving God with all your heart, and your neighbour as yourself. Or, as the Sikh teacher, Guru Nanak, said, 'To love God you must first learn to love one another.'

So, you have a great deal of learning and living to do on the journey ahead of you. Don't go through it blindfolded, without thinking for yourself. Be alert, be aware! Take a good look in the mirror and ask yourself:

Remember to keep three things in mind as you work out your own views:

- Always try to make some kind of sense out of your life – have a direction and a purpose.
- Think hard about what things are important to you in life, and value them.
- Remember that there are other people besides you – take a thought for their feelings too.

Now, let's move on to the journey of life, starting with birth!

For discussion

1. Do you think the universe happened by chance, or for a purpose?
2. Do you think there is life on other planets, or other universes?
3. In what ways do you think animals can show that they are intelligent? How does humankind differ from other animals?

Quick questions

1. How old is the Earth, how many stars are there in the Milky Way, and how many galaxies do we know of?
2. What is meant by the Big Bang in modern science?
3. What two things about the universe make scientists think that the Big Bang happened?
4. Scientists have two ideas of what there might have been before the Big Bang. What are these ideas?
5. What chemicals are needed for life to form, and when did the first living things appear on Earth?
6. When did *homo habilis* live, and how human was he/she?
7. What is the name of the species that we belong to, and how long has our species been on Earth for?
8. There are two reasons why humankind is the dominant species. What are they?
9. What responsibilities does this give us?

What's the point of it all?

Read through the picture-strip where the boy and the girls are talking. What reasons do some of them give for thinking that there is a meaning to life? What reasons are given for thinking that there is no meaning? What do *you* think?

Tell me a story!

Read through the information on the creation stories and answer the following questions:

1. Did ancient people think the world was formed by accident?
2. What does Tiamat stand for in the Marduk story, and what does the water stand for in the Genesis story?
3. What is the basic idea behind both these stories?
4. Who wrote down the Bible story and when, roughly? Were they men of science?
5. Do people who believe in God today think the world was made in six days?

Passing through

1. Why is life like a journey?
2. What are 'rites of passage'? How do these help us in life?
3. What happens to us if we can find no sense or purpose in our lives?
4. What do you want out of life?

Working it out

1. Write out the six ways that people have of trying to work out what is right and wrong. Give a brief example for each one.
2. Which of these is the most mature? Give reasons.
3. What basic rules can be followed when trying to work out what is right and wrong?
4. What do you need to do to work out your own morals?
5. Why do some religious people treat their scriptures and moral codes as rules that cannot be questioned, and why do some treat them more as guidelines?
6. What moral ideal do all religions have in common?
7. Read through the Ten Commandments in the Bible, Exodus 20:3–17. List the Commandments that are to do with God, and those that are to do with other people. Do you think that all of these should still apply today?

15

2 BIRTH

When a male sperm reaches an egg (ovum) in a female and fuses with it, then it is fertilised. If it implants in the womb, then it will develop, stage by stage, into a human child. It used to be thought that the personality or soul of the child entered it a stage later than conception, and the first signs of this were when the mother felt it move within her. Most people now think that it is fully alive from the moment of fertilisation, although some think that it only becomes a person in its own right when its brain starts to work. Nothing enters the child later on, though; it simply unfolds stage by stage.

After about 25 days, the baby's heart starts beating.

By the 7th week, the spine is formed and the rudimentary brain is completed. The foetus is about 6 mm long.

By the 8th week, the lungs are formed but they are still solid, arms and legs have appeared and there are holes for nostrils.

By the 11th week, the fingers and toes are distinguishable.

By the 13th week, the baby is fully formed.

By the 15th week, its fingers can curl and make fists.

By the 21st week, the first signs of hair appear. The foetus is about 30 cm long and weighs about 1 lb.

At 28 weeks, the foetus is viable – it has good chances of survival if born prematurely.

Twelve weeks later, the child is ready to be born.

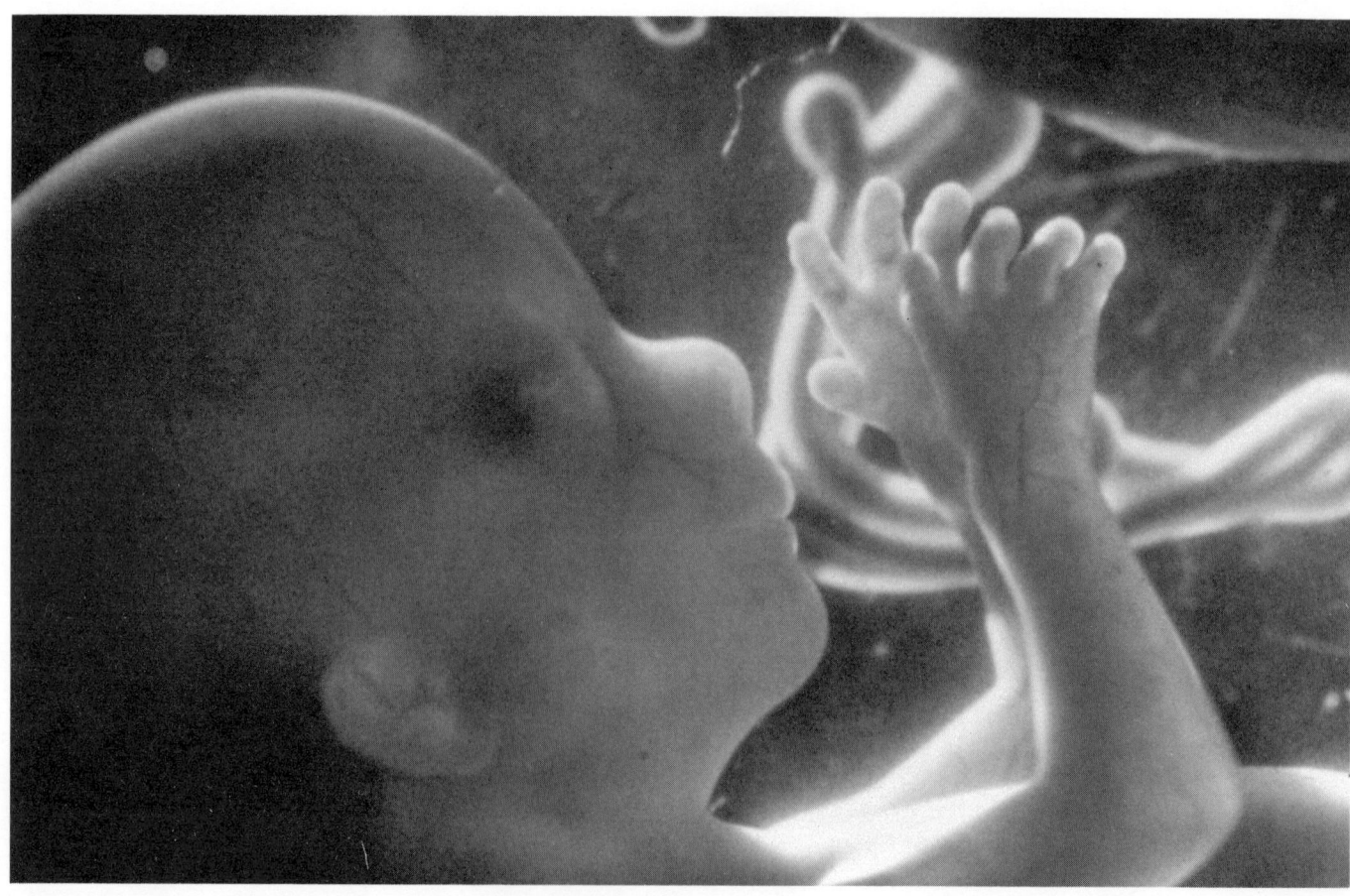

16

A baby inherits genes from both parents. Genes are minute particles that contain the information that decides the colour of your hair, your eyes and so on. Thus you will be like both your parents in different ways, but your genetic code, the arrangement of genes that forms your blueprint in the womb, is unique. There is no other code exactly like it. You are one of a kind! You are similar to your parents and other relatives, but you are also different. You have your own thoughts and feelings, and no one else in all of history will be exactly like you.

This means that you are special; if anything happens to you, you cannot be replaced. So, think of yourself as being something like a priceless work of art, that no one can set a value to!

You are thinking, feeling people. You have personalities that are unique and special. You are not just physical beings made up of atoms and chemicals. We do not really understand what makes all this work. Some people think that we each have an immortal soul (*immortal* = lasts for ever) that is joined with our physical bodies at the moment of conception, or shortly afterwards when the brain is active. Others think that our minds are just a result of the chemicals and electrical processes in our brains, like being a very advanced computer that can think for itself. This cannot be proved either way, but even if our minds are just part of our brains, our thoughts and feelings are still special and full of meaning. We can see, for example, that someone is happy if they are smiling, but we cannot see the happiness itself, just its results. It might be possible to measure the amount of electricity in the brain and to list the types of chemicals present when someone feels happy, but are you measuring the happiness itself, or the physical things that allow it to happen? Happiness is more than the physical things that happen when we feel happy; it is something in its own right, something spiritual as well as physical.

We can take an animal or a plant and study it to see that it moves and feeds and so is alive. We can then cut them up to see how they work, but we cannot extract the life from them and put it into a test-tube. We can see the signs that something is alive, but we cannot see life itself, just as we cannot see happiness in itself. Life is caused by physical things – atoms, chemicals, electricity – but it is more than these. It is something in its own right. Life is deep and mysterious, just like the universe we live in. Scientists have discovered many things about the universe, but there are probably many, many more things to discover. One famous scientist once said that he felt like a child finding pebbles in puddles on the beach, but there was still a huge ocean out there to explore!

Life is a mystery and a joy. The birth of a child is usually the cause for celebration in a family.

When parents first have their own children, they often say that they are amazed as they look at the tiny life that has come from both of them. It is wonderful, and fills you with awe to see a new life before your eyes! Relatives and friends will send the parents gifts and cards, and the parents may throw a party, inviting their friends to welcome the new life into the world and to share their joy.

Different cultures have different customs for welcoming a new life into the family. Religion often plays a part in these customs. Religious people value the birth of a child because life is seen as something from God; something extra-special that is to be cherished. Life is sacred. The child and its parents will be prayed for and blessed, and it will also be hoped that the child will carry on following its parents' faith as it grows older. Thus the birth of a child will be seen by a religious family as a way of allowing that faith to grow in the future, as they nurture the child in that faith and try to set it a good example.

In the picture-strip pages that follow, various birth rites will be covered, of Hinduism, Sikhism, Judaism, Christianity and Islam. The rites are as follows:

Hinduism – A service of naming and blessing, plus head shaving.

Sikhism – A service of thanksgiving and working out a name from their holy book.

Judaism – The rite of circumcision, with blessings.

Christianity – The rite of baptism.

Islam – Thanksgiving prayers at Tahneek, and hair clipping and circumcision at Aqeeqah.

HINDUISM

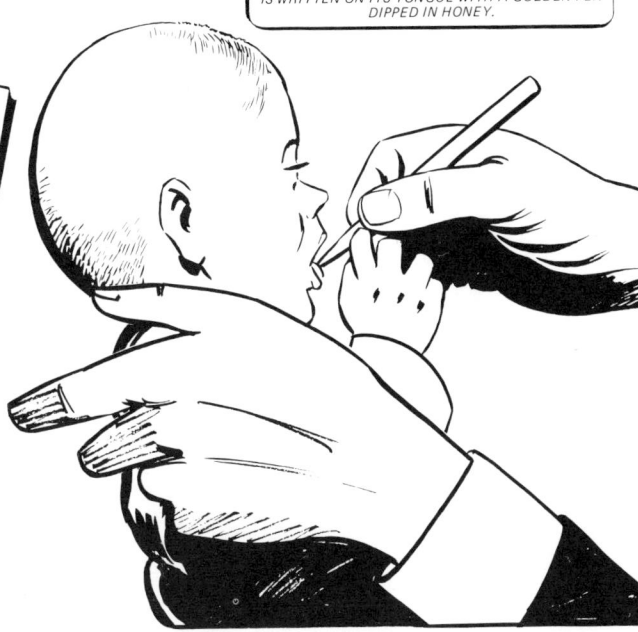

HINDUS HAVE A SPECIAL RITUAL FOR EVERY STAGE THAT WE GO THROUGH IN LIFE. THEY ARE CALLED SAMSKARAS. ONE OF THESE TAKES PLACE WHEN THE CHILD IS IN THE WOMB. THE WOMAN HAS PRAYERS SAID FOR HER, SHE READS HOLY SCRIPTURES AND EATS SPECIAL FOODS TO KEEP HER HEALTHY.

SOON AFTER THE BIRTH OF THE BABY IT IS BATHED AND THEN THE SACRED SYLLABLE, AUM, IS WRITTEN ON ITS TONGUE WITH A GOLDEN PEN DIPPED IN HONEY.

THE AUM SYLLABLE IS CHANTED IN PRAYER AND MEDITATION. IT STANDS FOR GOD, BREATH, LIFE AND PEACE.

THE PRIEST AT THE TEMPLE IS TOLD THE EXACT DATE AND TIME OF BIRTH, AND HE WORKS OUT A HOROSCOPE FROM THIS, AND SUGGESTS CERTAIN SYLLABLES FOR ITS NAME TO BE BASED ON. A SPECIAL, CEREMONIAL FOOD IS SHARED AROUND, CALLED PRASADAM, WHICH THE PRIEST HAS SPECIALLY BLESSED.

ALL HINDU BABIES HAVE THEIR HAIR SHAVED OFF SOON AFTER THEY HAVE GONE ON TO SOLID FOODS. HINDUS BELIEVE THAT PEOPLE LIVE MANY LIVES BY BEING CONSTANTLY REINCARNATED. THE ACT OF SHAVING THE HAIR SYMBOLISES THE STRIPPING AWAY OF ANY SINS GAINED IN THE PAST LIFE. THIS IS CALLED MUNDAN.

SIKHISM

SOON AFTER THE BIRTH OF A SIKH BABY, THE WORDS OF THE MOOL MANTRA WILL BE WHISPERED IN ITS EAR. THIS IS A VERY IMPORTANT SIKH PRAYER WHICH SUMS UP ALL THEIR BELIEFS ABOUT GOD.

THERE IS ONE GOD, ETERNAL TRUTH IS HIS NAME; MAKER OF ALL THINGS, PRESENT IN ALL THINGS. FEARING NOTHING AND AT ENMITY WITH NOTHING, TIMELESS IS HIS IMAGE; NOT MADE, SELF-EXISTING: BY THE GRACE OF THE GURU, MADE KNOWN TO MEN.

A FEW WEEKS LATER, THE FAMILY GOES TO THE TEMPLE, THE GURDWARA, TO OFFER THANKS TO GOD. THEY WILL PROVIDE THE FLOUR, SUGAR AND GHEE (CLARIFIED BUTTER) FOR THE PARSHAD, A SPECIAL FOOD THAT IS SHARED OUT. THEY WILL USUALLY OFFER AN EMBROIDERED COVER, CALLED A ROMALLA, FOR THE TEMPLE'S HOLY BOOK.

INSIDE THE TEMPLE THEY WILL GATHER IN FRONT OF THEIR HOLY BOOK, THE GRANTH, WHICH RESTS UNDER A CANOPY. PRAYERS WILL BE SAID AS SUGAR AND WATER ARE MIXED TOGETHER IN A BOWL.

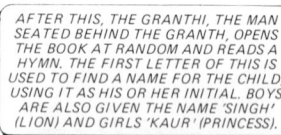

THIS MIXTURE IS DRIPPED INTO THE BABY'S MOUTH FROM THE END OF A KIRPAN, A CEREMONIAL SWORD. THE MOTHER DRINKS THE REST.

AFTER MORE PRAYERS HAVE BEEN SAID, THE PARSHAD IS SHARED OUT TO ALL THE WORSHIPPERS PRESENT.

AFTER THIS, THE GRANTHI, THE MAN SEATED BEHIND THE GRANTH, OPENS THE BOOK AT RANDOM AND READS A HYMN. THE FIRST LETTER OF THIS IS USED TO FIND A NAME FOR THE CHILD, USING IT AS HIS OR HER INITIAL. BOYS ARE ALSO GIVEN THE NAME 'SINGH' (LION) AND GIRLS 'KAUR' (PRINCESS).

JUDAISM

ISLAM

Step by step!

Draw a frame in your books and copy the information about the stages of development of a child in the womb into it.

Make sure you understand what the following words mean: **ovum, fertilisation, conception**.

New arrivals!

1. Why do you think that families celebrate the arrival of a new baby? Under what circumstances do you think a family might not feel like celebrating a new arrival?
2. Can you think of any ways your family or your relatives have of celebrating the arrival of a new baby?

Congratulations!

Read through the picture-strip section on the different rites that religions use to celebrate the birth of a child, and then answer the following:

1. Choose any two of the faiths mentioned on the picture-strip pages and find out how they express joy and thanksgiving at the birth of a child.
2. *Either*, compare the Christian practice of baptism with the rites of one other faith, mentioning similarities and differences.
   Or, find any information you can, from each faith, about the following and how they are used in the rites: WATER, LIGHT, SUGAR, HONEY, WINE, FOOD, PRAYER, HAIR, NAMES.

3 GROWING UP

Look at the children in the photograph, and think back to when you were that age. Life was fairly straightforward. Your parent, or parents, looked after you; you were fed, clothed and had a roof over your head. Things might still be the same in that respect today. Your family tries to provide food, clothing and shelter. Think how things have changed, though. When you were a child, did you have much say in what you were given to eat, or in what clothes were bought for you? Could you come and go from home as you wished? When your family went out, did you have to go with them?

You will probably still be living at home, under the same roof, but thinking, and feeling, and acting very differently. Your family should be treating you differently, also. This chapter is going to explore what is involved in all the changes of 'growing up'.

Over the last few years your bodies will have been going through some major changes.

Girls will have changed in the following ways:

- legs and torso lengthen
- waist narrows, hips grow rounder, pads of fat develop around thighs
- the breasts develop, hair grows under the arms and pubic hair appears
- the fertility cycle starts to operate, and **menstruation** begins (= 'periods' – these start, on average, when girls are 12–13)

These changes are caused by **hormones** being released in the body. These are **oestrogen** and **progesterone** in girls.

Boys will have gone through the following changes:

- legs lengthen, the muscles develop
- the shoulders broaden out, and the waist narrows
- hair starts to grow under the arms, on the face, and pubic hair appears around the penis
- the voice goes lower (or 'breaks') because the larynx (voice box) grows larger, forming the 'Adam's apple'

These changes are also caused by hormones, called *androgens* in boys.

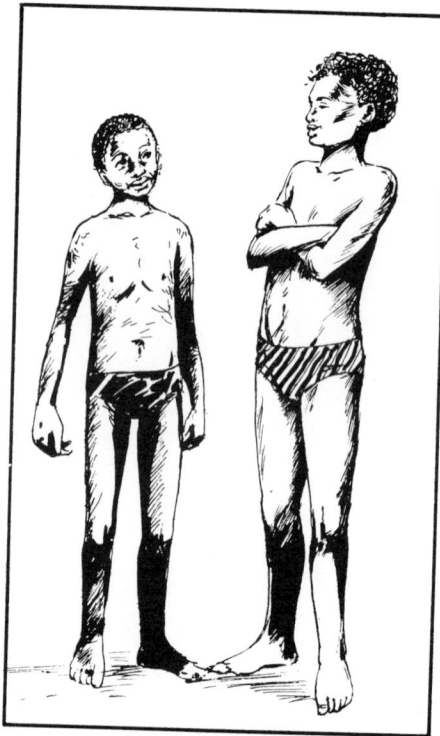

No doubt the effect of these changes has been great enough – wondering what was happening, being embarrassed by voice changes, clumsiness as limbs developed, but the inner, emotional changes you have been going through seem even greater! The most obvious emotional change is that you are aware of sex – a delicate subject, and we will hear more about that later! Many other changes have taken place, though, that might be much more confusing in a way.

I want to be me!

Growing up means growing to be more and more independent of your parent or parents. Whereas they used to do nearly everything for you, you are starting to have more responsibility for your own life. You had to learn how to feed yourself and how to dress yourself when you were a young child, and during your teens you have to learn how to think for yourself in a whole variety of ways. What you are saying to yourself, all the time, is 'I want to be me!', and you cannot be yourself until you let go of the proverbial apron strings!

The problem is that you are not sure who 'me' really is, yet. You are launching out, breaking more free of your family, trying to work out your ideas and feelings about many things. You are going through a period of change, trying many things and ideas out for size. You might change friends and interests, and opinions about life, sport, politics and religion many times. This will annoy many adults who tend to have their ideas about things more worked out, and thus they are more settled. Don't let this trouble you, though; it is perfectly natural, and it will take some time before you settle down more. (Not usually until after your teens, perhaps in your twenties!)

CONFLICTS!

ALL THE CHANGES YOU ARE GOING THROUGH CAN LEAD TO MANY!

You are trying to sort out your own ideas and your own identity. It helps to listen to what other people are saying, and share your thoughts and your feelings with friends of your own age. Some parents will not be very understanding, partly because many things have changed in society since they were younger – there are new ideas about fashion and music around, for example; they might have gone through very similar things, though, if only they are honest and think back to when they were younger, but they might find it hard to admit it! Even if you have a parent or parents who are very understanding, you will still find that there are things you cannot talk to them about that you can say to your friends. This is why teenagers like to go out as much as possible and join various groups. You need the experience, and the chance to 'let it all hang out' away from the watching eyes of adults.

You might want to join a particular fashion, or follow a particular type of music, to feel that you belong. You are going through a time when you are 'letting go' of your parent or parents, and trying to find a new identity, separate from your family. Joining a group helps you to do this because you are putting a new identity tag on.

Belonging to a particular group gives you friends, a new identity, and a feeling of security – of having somewhere to go where you belong.

Heroes!

When you are trying to sort your feelings out, it helps some people to follow a striking personality that you think you would like to imitate. You follow heroes who appeal to you, and give you strong ideas about how to live. These ideas could be about dress, politics, music, sex, sport, religion or other aspects of general life-style. The most common heroes and heroines among teenagers are pop stars. This has been the case, probably, since the 1950s, and for some years before that it would have been the movie stars. These are all daring, larger than life characters. Politicians can figure too, especially ones with new ideas that promise to change things in society. Teenagers go through so many changes, that people with new ideas appeal – they are trendsetters, and not seen as 'bores'. Outrageous figures appeal to some teenagers because these characters shock their parents and help teenagers form their own, separate identities, different from their parents.

Look at the following photographs and think what ideas you get from each one about how to live your life.

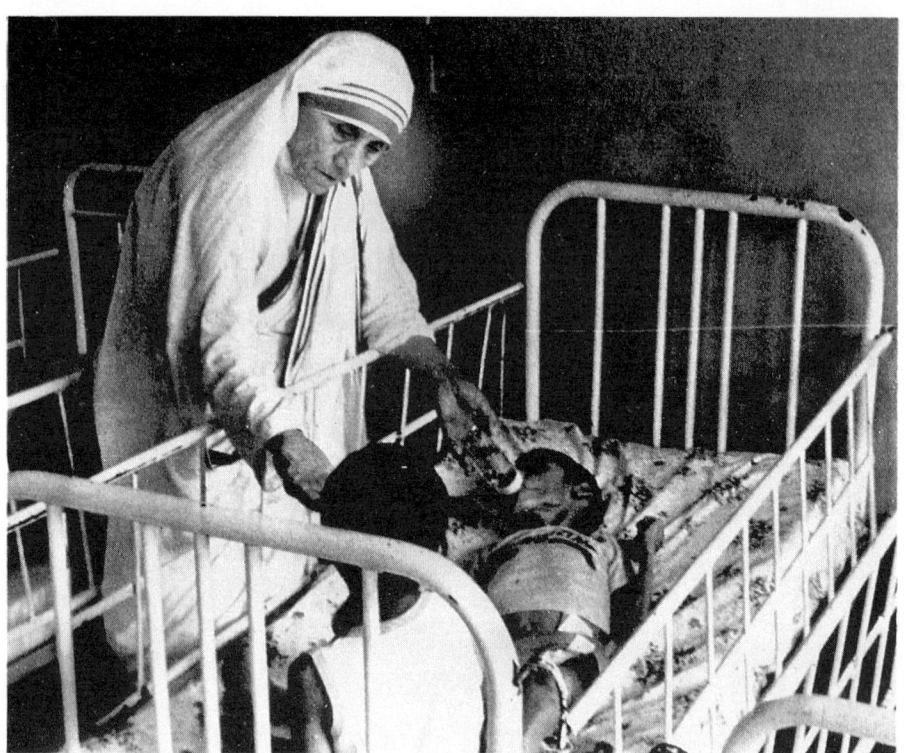
Mother Teresa

David Bowie

Viv Richards

A teenager is trying to find his or her own feet, his or her own identity in life. Spending more time with friends than with your family, listening to a certain type of music, and dressing in clothes that *you* choose, all help you to do this. Yet to some teenagers there are even more important ways than these of showing that they are growing up.

Some teenagers start to smoke when they are with their friends. This makes them feel that they have crossed a threshold – this is something only adults do! It makes them feel 'big', and they might not be accepted in their group if they do not.

Drinking alcohol with friends, especially at parties – getting drunk can be a way of showing off and helps people to feel that they have left their childhood behind.

Going out with members of the opposite sex becomes more and more important, not just in groups with other friends, but on a one-to-one basis. These could be just good friendships, or they could include sexual experience – this, again, might make teenagers feel they had left childhood behind and crossed a threshold.

Some boys feel more grown-up by saving up and buying a motorcycle of some sort. This gives them even more independence, and the new responsibility of learning to drive it carefully makes them feel they have crossed that threshold.

Another important way of feeling grown-up is to get a part-time job and earn some money for yourself, not having to rely on your parents giving you pocket-money. This gives you more confidence and independence.

These are just some of the ways in which young people feel they have crossed a threshold. Not everything in these examples *really* shows that they are becoming more adult. Growing up into adulthood means forming ideas of your own, and becoming responsible for your own life; this involves a good deal of discipline and care. Being responsible for your own life means being thoughtful about the feelings of others. Some teenage ideas of being 'grown-up' are really very irresponsible and are just ways of letting off steam and trying to be accepted by their friends. Look through the examples again: which do you think are true ways of showing that you are growing up?

Smoking

Why do some people smoke cigarettes? They might start smoking for a number of reasons:

1. **To feel grown-up** – this is something they have not been allowed to do as children, and they might want to if their parents do and if their friends do.
2. **So they don't feel left out** – if most of their friends are smoking, then they might feel odd if they refuse to. Will they be laughed at?
3. **To make them look 'hard'** – some people might think that it shows they are 'one of the boys', or 'one of the girls' if they smoke.
4. **To calm their nerves** – cigarettes can help to soothe tensions in people when they are under stress or are worried.

Cigarettes are addictive. This is because of a drug in them called nicotine. Your body will get used to this, and you will feel irritable and depressed if you go without a cigarette for a few days. Some people also depend on them to help them get through the day, to calm nerves. This is why most people find it very hard to stop smoking, especially if they start when they are young.

The nicotine is not the sole factor that damages health, though. It is also the minute amounts of tar that pass into the lungs as the cigarette is smoked. These build up into a lining in the lungs that can cause difficulties with breathing, chest complaints and can contribute to lung cancer. Some gases in the tobacco can also damage your health.

Your motto should be to think this through for yourself; do you want to become dependent on nicotine and risk damaging your lungs, heart and stomach? Is it worth feeling part of a 'gang' for you to do this?

Drinking

Many people enjoy a social drink of alcohol or a quiet drink at home. It can taste pleasant, feels warm inside and relaxes the nerves. For most people, that is where it ends.

Some people become alcohol dependent, though. This means that they can't get through the day without a few drinks to relax them and steady their nerves. If their problem becomes worse, then they become alcoholic, and they are addicted. They need medical help to 'dry out', to allow the alcohol to pass through their bloodstream, and they need counselling, too. People develop these problems either through excessive drinking, perhaps in order to be 'one of the gang', or through emotional problems, where the release that alcohol gives is all too welcome!

Most people do not become dependent or alcoholic. Some teenagers like to experiment with alcohol, and getting drunk can be one of their ways of feeling 'grown-up'. Most will outgrow this excessive drinking and calm down as they grow older. Some might run a risk of becoming too dependent, however, especially if they start very young. Even if they don't develop such problems, one drink too many can get you into all kinds of trouble:

- You might become aggressive and hurt someone, and you will deeply regret it when you are sober.
- You might be run over because you were fooling about on a road, or you might cause the driver to swerve and crash.
- You might go too far with a member of the opposite sex and regret it later – especially if a girl becomes pregnant!
- You might damage your liver and make your body unhealthy.

So, your motto should be, 'Think before you drink!'

EAST MEETS WEST

Rites of initiation

The basic problem teenagers face in Western society is that they are in an in-between stage. They are no longer children, but not yet adults. They are not quite sure what they are, and adults are not quite sure how to react to them.

This problem is clear in our society when you study the Law. The Law says:

- You can have a part-time job at 13.
- You can enter a public house at 14, but you cannot drink any alcohol.
- You can marry at 16 with your parent or parents' permission. 16 is also the legal age for sexual relations.
- You can learn to drive at 17.
- At 18 you can vote and consume alcohol in public.

So, you can be married, but still not be able to vote or go out for a drink to a pub, until you are 18! At 18 you 'come of age', and you are officially an adult. This used to be at 21, and then you were handed 'the key of the door', meaning that you could come and go from home as you pleased!

It is a great pity that there are no official 'thresholds' that you can pass over until you are 18. It is true that sitting exams, like the 16-plus, are a threshold, ending your school life; and getting your first job is another significant step. Yet you are not considered to be a responsible adult until you are 18 and there are various legal restraints on you until then, as has been seen.

This might be why teenagers feel they have to go through so much rebellion, to make sure their thoughts and feelings are heard and taken notice of. This

might be why some people experiment with smoking, heavy drinking and sex, to convince themselves that they are growing up, as well as to convince their parents.

In other cultures there are special ceremonies which help you pass from childhood to adulthood, and they happen much earlier than at 18! These ceremonies are called 'rites of initiation'. You have to perform a special act as a part of the ceremony, and this shows that you have passed on to another stage in the journey of life. These cultures are usually very religious, and prayers are said, asking God to guide the young person through life, and to bless him or her as they grow up. God is thought to go with you on every step in life's journey, starting you off and then leading you on. For religious people, the coming of age of their children is a great joy, because it shows that they have fully accepted their parents' religion and way of life. It is interesting to note that such cultures have far fewer teenage problems!

The following pages will explore the rites of initiation of some of the major world faiths:

Hinduism – the Sacred Thread ceremony
Sikhism – the Amrit ceremony
Judaism – Bar Mitzvah or Bat Mitzvah
Christianity – Confirmation
Islam – prayer and fasting

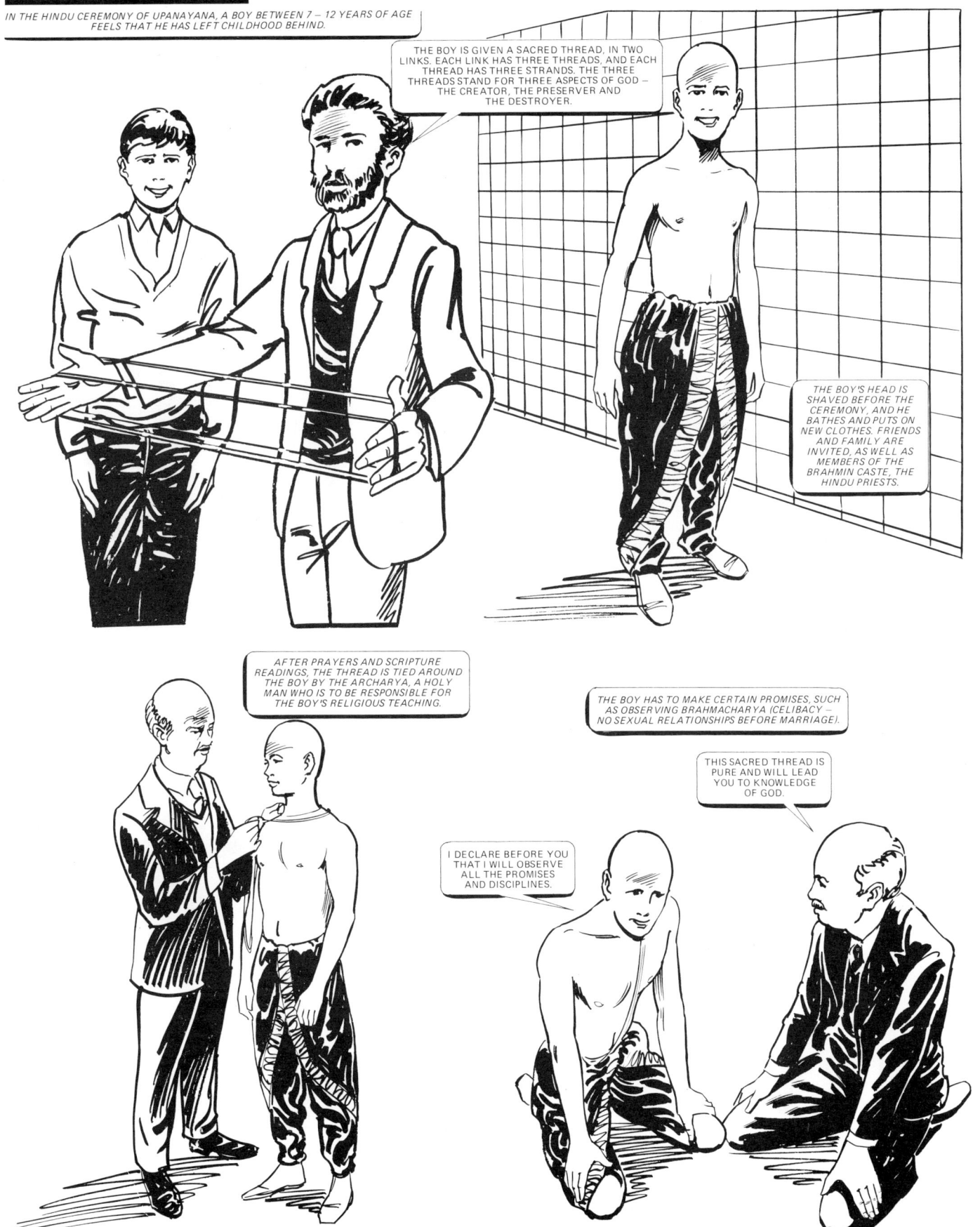

HINDUISM

IN THE HINDU CEREMONY OF UPANAYANA, A BOY BETWEEN 7 – 12 YEARS OF AGE FEELS THAT HE HAS LEFT CHILDHOOD BEHIND.

THE BOY IS GIVEN A SACRED THREAD, IN TWO LINKS. EACH LINK HAS THREE THREADS, AND EACH THREAD HAS THREE STRANDS. THE THREE THREADS STAND FOR THREE ASPECTS OF GOD – THE CREATOR, THE PRESERVER AND THE DESTROYER.

THE BOY'S HEAD IS SHAVED BEFORE THE CEREMONY, AND HE BATHES AND PUTS ON NEW CLOTHES. FRIENDS AND FAMILY ARE INVITED, AS WELL AS MEMBERS OF THE BRAHMIN CASTE, THE HINDU PRIESTS.

AFTER PRAYERS AND SCRIPTURE READINGS, THE THREAD IS TIED AROUND THE BOY BY THE ARCHARYA, A HOLY MAN WHO IS TO BE RESPONSIBLE FOR THE BOY'S RELIGIOUS TEACHING.

THE BOY HAS TO MAKE CERTAIN PROMISES, SUCH AS OBSERVING BRAHMACHARYA (CELIBACY – NO SEXUAL RELATIONSHIPS BEFORE MARRIAGE).

THIS SACRED THREAD IS PURE AND WILL LEAD YOU TO KNOWLEDGE OF GOD.

I DECLARE BEFORE YOU THAT I WILL OBSERVE ALL THE PROMISES AND DISCIPLINES.

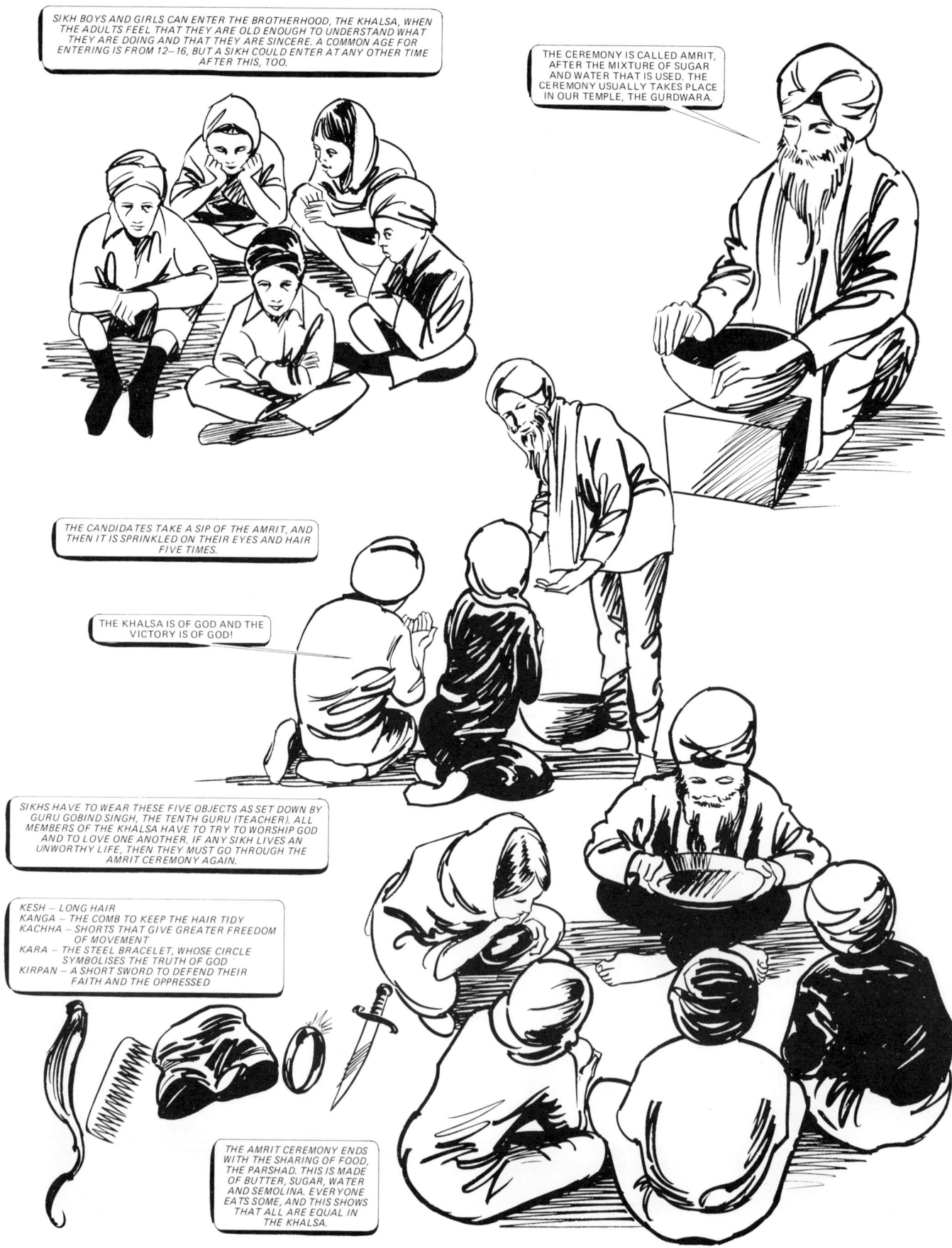

Those were the days!

List any things you can think of that are different now from when you were a child, e.g.:

Child
I was born into my family.

Teenager
I choose my own friends.

and so on . . .

Body building!

Read through the pages on how your body has changed. Then write a paragraph on how you have changed, including any of your memories and any amusing incidents!

Battleground!

1. Discuss some of the situations on the picture-strip pages, 'Conflicts!', in the class. Can you think of any other situations where conflicts might arise between you and adults?
2. Write a paragraph putting yourself into the shoes of one of your parents and say how you think they might feel, and why, in one of the situations mentioned, or perform a short role-play, with a friend, one of you being the teenager and one the parent.

A friend indeed!

1. What sort of people do you make friends with? What qualities do you look for in a friend? What sort of things can you talk to friends about that you can't talk to parents about?
2. Can you talk to parents about some things that you can't talk to friends about?
3. What qualities do you look for in a member of the opposite sex whom you want to go out with?

What, me?

Plan and write out a character profile of how you see yourself as an adult. Use the following headings: APPEARANCE, DRESS, CAREER, HOBBIES AND INTERESTS, EXCITING EXPERIENCES.

One step beyond!

1. What things make you feel that you have crossed a threshold from childhood to adulthood?
2. Think up a good rite of initiation that our society could use to make you feel more adult at an age earlier than 18. What age would this take place at? What would you have to do?

Smoking and drinking

1. Think of as many reasons as you can why people start smoking.
2. Think of as many reasons as you can why some people refuse to smoke.
3. Why do smokers find it hard to stop smoking cigarettes?
4. How might smoking damage a person's health?
5. Why do most people enjoy a social drink?
6. What do you think makes some people get drunk regularly?
7. What is the difference between alcohol dependence and alcoholism?
8. What dangers can heavy drinking lead to?

With God by your side . . .

Read through the section on 'Rites of initiation'.

1. What difference do you think a belief in God makes to people when they are growing up?
2. When young people of the religions mentioned perform the rites, their circumstances change. Find out what new responsibilities each child has and list them. Then say, in your opinion, which rites make a person feel the most grown-up.
3. Take one of the rites you have selected, and write a few paragraphs putting yourself in the position of the young person. Say what happens and how you feel.
4. What problems do you think an Asian young girl or boy might have being brought up in a Western country?

4 SEX

Patterning?

The physical differences between boys and girls are obvious, but are they different mentally and emotionally? If we study the way that boys and girls are brought up, this will tell us what many people think. Look at the list below, and select what you would buy for a young girl, and then for a young boy:

> Toy soldiers   A football
> A toy rolling-pin   A train set
> A toy gun   A doll   A cowboy suit   A nurse's uniform

This will show your attitudes to what type of personalities boys and girls are supposed to have. It is usually thought that girls are more emotional and sensitive than boys; they cry more easily. It is usually thought that men are stronger than women, so they should be the ones who go out to work and fight in a war. So little girls are usually given things like dolls and toy rolling-pins and nurses' uniforms, because they are brought up to be caring, to look after a home, or to look after other people. Little boys are often given guns and soldiers because they are supposed to be tougher and more aggressive. Football is for boys because this takes physical strength and an ability to get involved in rough-and-tumble. Yet how true is all this? Perhaps little children are patterned from birth to fit into certain roles. If you are given a gun to play with, perhaps you will show more aggression than if you were given a doll. You will think it is perfectly all right for you to show aggression, and so you do.

If you were given dolls to play with, then you would think that you were expected to be caring and gentle. If boys were given

41

dolls, and girls were given guns, would they grow up differently?

This patterning can also be seen in childhood when little boys are told off for crying in public, but little girls would be patted on the head! Perhaps boys are just as emotional as girls, but they have been brought up to keep their feelings hidden much more.

Patterning can carry on through life. Look at the four pictures on the right and see what they tell you about putting boys and girls into fixed roles:

Do you think the boy could change places with the girl in the pictures?

Now look at these four pictures; do you think there is anything wrong with men and women doing these jobs?

The traditional way of bringing boys and girls up is called **patriarchy**, where men are the heads of the home and are the leaders in the country. This has been slowly changing in recent years, with more women going out to work and finding a career, and more women taking jobs that used to be for men only. Some families work best if the man stays at home and looks after the children, while the wife goes out to work!

At the turn of the century, there were no women MPs, and women could not vote, but the 1980s have seen a woman Prime Minister!

Perhaps there is not such a great difference between boys

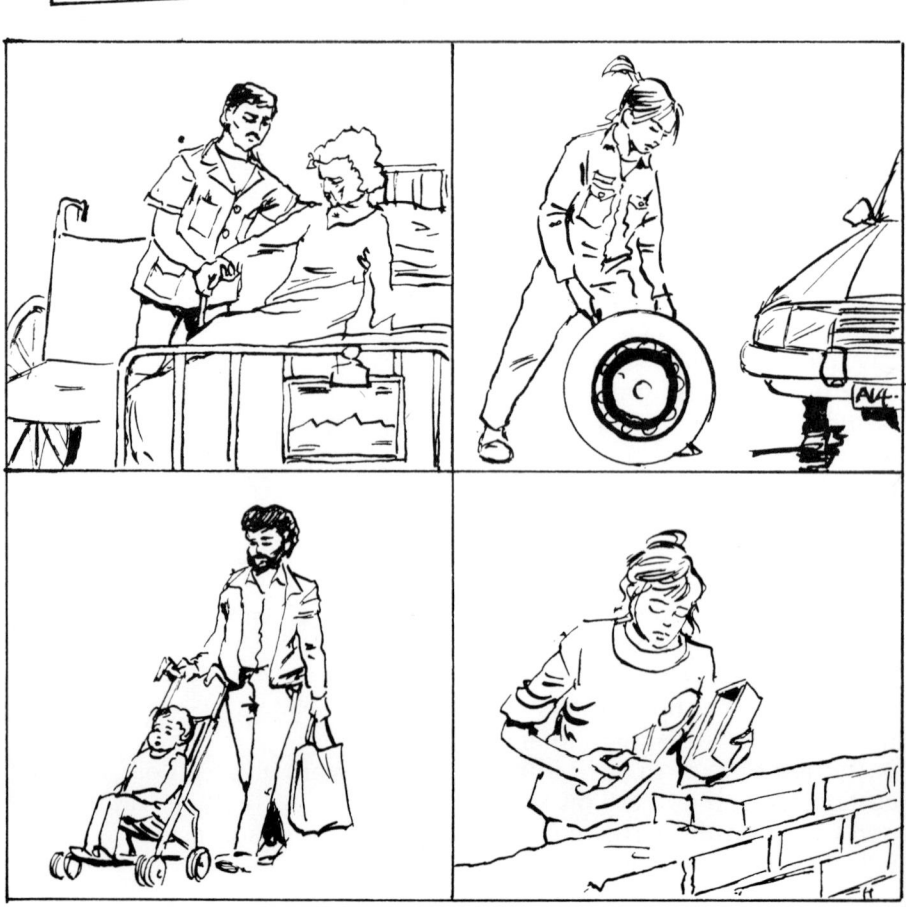

and girls, emotionally and mentally, after all! Yet many people still behave as though there were. When boys act tough and dare not admit to any weakness in front of their friends, this is a sign of patterning; again, they may feel like crying, but they dare not do so because of the way they have been brought up. The macho-men heroes in the films, such as Roger Moore as 'James Bond', Clint Eastwood as 'The Man with No Name' or Sylvester Stallone as 'Rocky' or 'Rambo', are other examples of the power of patriarchy that is still around in our society.

More and more people are questioning patriarchy, though, and are trying to work out their own roles, from male pop stars who wear dresses and make-up, to young families sharing roles and jobs in the house; it is no longer always the woman's work to clean or to cook.

Boys are not necessarily any stronger or more intelligent than girls but males and females are still very different in many ways! Girls will react to some things differently from boys, and their emotional make-up is influenced quite a bit by their fertility cycle and menstruation. They are geared up to be child-bearers, whether they choose to have children or not. The danger to avoid is putting boys and girls into fixed roles or stereotypes that do not completely suit them.

Sexuality

Physical differences between boys and girls are the most obvious, though, and in the past few years you will have become aware of sexual feelings. The boys who used to find the girls annoying are now attracted to them! Sexuality, when it starts to awaken, is probably the most delicate and stormy area in a person's development. Sexual feeling is perfectly natural, and it might help to explore the idea of what sex is for.

The main reason for sex existing is so that we can reproduce the species. Amongst animals this is probably its only function. Of course, we do not know if animals enjoy sex in the sense of having fun and forming a close friendship, but the pattern of animal sexuality suggests that reproduction is the main point of it! The fertility cycle of most female animals is completely different from that of female humans. Many female animals, such as cats and dogs, are fertile for only short periods of each year, when they are said to be 'on heat'. They will emit a scent to attract males, and they might have sex with several males in their fertile period! This is to make sure that they get pregnant, for they will not have another chance until the following fertile period, and so nature ensures that they reproduce. If you have a female cat or dog then you will know how sexually active they will be when on heat, and how much of a nuisance they can be!

A female human's fertility cycle is different because she is fertile throughout the year. This gives humans one great advantage – they can afford to have the luxury of only having one sexual partner if they so choose. The same urgency to become pregnant is not there. That is not how we are made. This means that sex can take on new levels of meaning for humans. It is not just there to reproduce the species. It can involve pleasure, and it can also be a deep way of showing care and friendship.

When you are growing up, and you first become aware of sex, there will be a great deal of curiosity, and sharing of ideas and joking with friends. Young people have a variety of viewpoints about sex, but it is probably true that there is a good deal of pressure from friends to take a free-and-easy attitude, and boys will often boast about losing their virginity (whether in fact they have or not!).

It is often the case that a young person's attitude to sex depends upon that of the group of friends he or she has. Part of growing up is becoming more responsible for your own life, and it is not always easy to form your own opinions and stand out from the crowd.

Girls react differently from boys to sex. They respond to touch more readily and will usually only want to have sex with someone they care for and have a relationship with. Boys, on the other hand, are sexually aroused more quickly and might be more interested in the pleasure than the relationship.

Most young people will have relationships with members of the opposite sex when they are in their teens, and it is important to work out your own feelings and ideas about sex.

POINTS OF VIEW

There are so many different opinions about when it is right to have sex. Some young people, having just discovered sex, are eager to experiment, and think it is all just a bit of fun. They find it hard to understand why other people advise caution. There are three reasons for being very careful about sex.

1. Sex involves people

Sex should be more than a personal pleasure. If it is not, then it is selfish. Sex should be about sharing, about a very intimate act between two people. People are not objects; they have feelings, and sexual feelings are very sensitive and delicate. People can easily be hurt by someone abusing them sexually. Sex should never be forced upon anyone, as Gary was trying to do to Jenny in the picture-strip. Also, if people are too free and easy about having sex, they might find it very hard to settle down in a marriage. So, if sex is not part of a meaningful relationship, problems might follow!

2. If you're not careful, sex can make babies!

Sex is not just about fun and friendship; it is also about reproduction! If you do decide to have sex, it is important to seek advice on contraception to prevent an unwanted pregnancy occurring. Some young people do not bother, and think they will be all right the first time, but they are often wrong, and the girl becomes pregnant.

There are various types of contraception available:

For men: The sheath

The sheath, also called the condom or durex, is made out of thin rubber and is worn over the man's penis during intercourse. This stops the sperm from entering the vagina. It must be placed over the penis just prior to intercourse and removed afterwards. It cannot be reused. The sheath is a very reliable method so long as the container has the 'kite-mark' displayed on it. This is the sign that it is approved by the British Standards Institution.

Sterilisation

This is a final method of contraception that cannot be reversed. It is only for men who are certain that they do not want to have any more children. It involves a small operation called a vasectomy which blocks the tubes that carry the sperm.

For women: The pill

A contraceptive pill taken by the woman stops ovulation (the release of an egg) taking place each month by adding new hormones to the body. There are different types of pill available, and a doctor advises a woman on which he/she thinks will suit her best. The pill can be obtained from a doctor's surgery or from a Family Planning Clinic.

The pill is very reliable and easy to use, but there can be dangers. If young, teenage girls start taking the pill regularly, then they might run the risk of being infertile in later life. The pill can also cause health problems for women in later life who are smokers, are overweight, or have heart complaints. Another consideration is that it is easier to be taken advantage of by men when otherwise you might have thought twice about having sex!

The coil

The IUD (intrauterine device) is a piece of plastic or plastic wound with copper that is about 2–4 cm long. It is placed in the womb by the doctor, and should be checked once or twice a year. This device works by stopping the egg from settling in the womb. It is a non-hormonal treatment that is reliable – it is estimated that two to four women out of every hundred that use it each year become pregnant. It can sometimes cause a mild cramp-like pain and heavy periods, but this does no harm.

The cap

This is a soft, rubber cap that comes in various sizes. (A larger size is called the diaphragm.) It is inserted in the vagina at first by a doctor, and its use is explained to the woman. It must be inserted before intercourse and kept in for six hours afterwards. It must be used with a contraceptive cream (spermicide), and the cap should be rinsed clean in warm, but not hot, water afterwards. The cap has no side-effects, and might even guard against cancer of the cervix. About three out of every

100 women that use it each year become pregnant.

Natural methods

A woman ovulates roughly midway between periods. The egg remains ready to be fertilised for about two days, and male sperm can survive for up to five days inside the woman's body. Therefore, the week in the middle of the menstrual cycle is the time when a woman is most likely to get pregnant if she has intercourse without contraception.

The natural methods of contraception try to work out when this fertile period occurs each month. There are four natural methods:

a. *The temperature method* – Body temperature usually drops at the time of ovulation, and rises afterwards. It is thought safe to have sex after three successive days at this higher temperature.

b. *The Billings method* – This works by checking for changes in the cervical mucus in the vagina. More discharge occurs four days prior to ovulation and continues during the fertile period. If a woman has sex after four days when the discharge is less, or drier, then it is thought to be safe.

c. *The calendar method* – This is where a woman tries to predict her fertile periods in advance by keeping a record of the length of her menstrual cycle for at least six months.

d. *A combination of methods* – To be extra careful, a woman might combine the above three methods.

This method avoids any side-effects, but it is not completely reliable. More unplanned pregnancies occur using this method than any other!

Injections

There are two types of contraceptive injection, and these are only recommended to women who cannot use other types of contraception. One gives protection for eight weeks, and the other for twelve weeks. These stop ovulation occuring, like the pill, and they are said to be 99 per cent effective. They can alter the frequency of a woman's periods, though.

Sterilisation

This is a final form of contraception for women who are certain that they do not want any more children. It involves a small operation where the tubes carrying the egg are blocked.

3. Medical problems

If someone has sex casually with a number of partners, then they are more likely to become infected by a type of sexually transmitted disease, such as gonorrhoea. This causes inflammation of the genitals, and it might make people sterile (unable to have children). Nearly all STD (Sexually Transmitted Diseases) can be cured if they are treated in their early stages. If one person is affected, then they will pass it on to anyone else they have sex with. (Note that STD can only be caught by having sexual relations with someone who has it.)

Another medical problem can be cancer of the cervix. The cervix is the neck of the woman's womb. This is very sensitive, especially in teenage years. The risk of cancer of the cervix is increased if a girl starts to have sex early in life, and if she has a number of different partners. The sheath might help to stop the development of cancer of the cervix or the spreading of STD.

So, human sexuality is very delicate and sensitive, and should be handled with care!

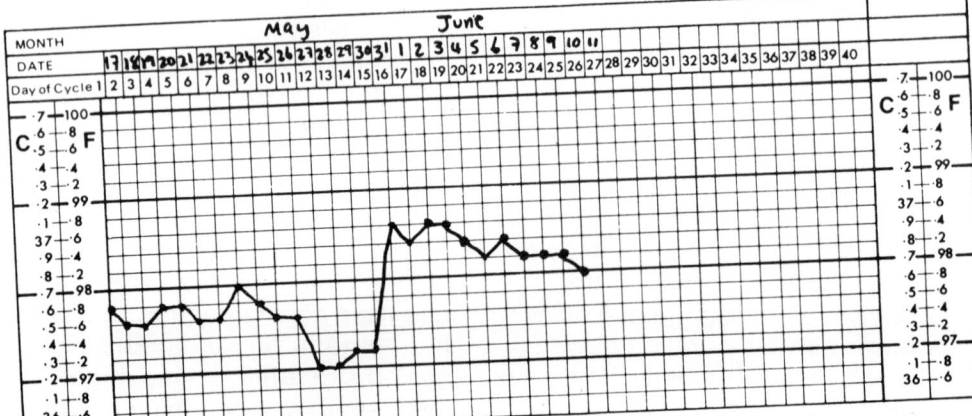

For a girl in Beccy's situation there are the three options – have the child and keep it; have the child and get it adopted; have the child aborted. Abortion might seem the easiest way out, but it is a very sensitive issue. Some girls are very depressed afterwards and often wonder what their child might have been like and they might feel guilty. Some people have very strong feelings about abortion. They say that it is like murder because the foetus in the womb is alive and will develop into a baby if undisturbed; the unborn child is defenceless and should be given rights in law. The Roman Catholic Church strongly opposes abortion, as do some other religious groups.

The Law allows abortion for any of four reasons, since 1967:

1. If the life of the mother is threatened by continuing with the pregnancy.
2. If her physical or mental health is threatened.
3. If her existing children would suffer as a result.
4. If there is a substantial risk that the child might be born severely handicapped.

Some people, including some religious people, feel that the foetus is not really a person in the early stages of growth in the womb before there is evidence of any brain activity. Hence it is all right to abort it then, but not later. The Law will allow abortions up to the foetus being 28 weeks old. Many pressure groups argue their case on either side; for example, SPUC (The Society for the Protection of Unborn Children) against, and ALRA (The Abortion Law Reform Association) for. (ALRA wants the 1967 law changed so that any woman can have an abortion on demand.)

5 MARRIAGE

What is marriage?

Why do people get married? Many people would probably say because they are in love. Marriages are seen as 'love matches' by most people in the West. Yet this is not how it has always been, and it is not how it is for some people in the world today. Some marriages are **arranged**. This means that a marriage is arranged by the couple's parents. Usually, however, the couple have the final word, and can refuse to marry each other. Marriages are arranged because the parents feel that they want the best for their children, and a suitor's personality, prospects and wealth may be taken into consideration.

Hindus, Sikhs and Muslims have arranged marriages. Although courting is forbidden, customs will vary from family to family. Some will encourage the couple to get to know each other before the wedding, and some couples will only meet occasionally. It used to be the custom in Hindu weddings that the couple only met on the wedding day itself, but this is not usually the case now.

Many Western people find the idea of arranged marriages hard to accept. It seems too planned and formal. How can the couple really know if they love each other? Hindus, Sikhs and Muslims would answer that the couple can grow to love each other in a working relationship, running a family. It is a fact that there are less divorces among

Asians, for example; perhaps the idea of 'working at a marriage' does strengthen the relationship. Western people prefer the freedom of choosing their own partners, and spending time with them before the wedding to get to know them properly. People who are used to arranged marriages fear that a marriage based just on good feelings will not be very secure. What if the people stop feeling that they are in love?

What makes Western people marry? Here are some things that might make people get married:

- Sexual attraction
- Good job prospects
- Your partner is friendly and easy to talk to
- You share the same interests
- Your partner has plenty of money
- You feel your partner understands you better than anyone else

- Which do you think are the most important reasons?
- Which ones would not be a very strong foundation for a marriage?
- What type of love should a marriage be based upon? Romantic stories often show a girl being swept off her feet by a tall, dark, handsome man and they live happily ever after. Attraction and friendship need to be very deep for a marriage to work out. You can like someone, 'fancy' someone, have a crush on someone, or be infatuated by them, but this does not necessarily mean that you *love* them! A basic question to ask yourself is:

them for losing a daughter. (One pair of hands less to do jobs around the house!)

Marriages were economic arrangements because the parents hoped to get something back from the deal. In the past, when there was no national welfare system, there was no government pension. Old people relied upon their children to look after them, and so it was essential to marry them off to good partners in order to have a strong family to support them in old age.

Which elements of a marriage do you think were more important in societies that worked like the ones mentioned above: companionship; having children; money; responsibility to parents; sexual attraction?

Marriage today

Western society has changed greatly in the last few centuries. We now have a welfare state system that gives out unemployment benefit, child benefit, free medical care on the National Health, and old age pensions. Do people still need to get married? There is not the same need to provide for parents in old age, or to have children to make sure you are looked after in turn. There is more contraception available, too, so that a couple could have frequent sex without the risk of producing children if they are careful. If you like someone, why not just live together?

How did marriage start?

Marriages were all probably arranged many years ago when humankind was first developing and settling down. A marriage was an economic arrangement – the parents could not afford to go on providing for the children, and so they wanted them to start their own families. Dowries in ancient times were paid to the bride's parents to compensate

Some people do try living together, and this works for them, but it can cause complications, particularly if they have any children. Another problem is that if any difficulties come along, such as unpaid bills, disagreements, and so on, it is more tempting for the couple to 'throw in the towel' and split up. Living together, in or out of marriage, is not easy. It is something you have to work at.

Marriages can break down; there is no guarantee of success with anyone, but an advantage of being married is that everything is 'signed and sealed'. It is harder to think of just walking out. You have made a commitment to each other, and in public. In wedding services, whether they are civil or religious, you have to take vows. Think of these as extra-strong promises. You agree to stay together through thick and thin, and to honour one another – that is the ideal, anyway! This helps people psychologically – they feel they have something to live up to.

So, there is not the same economic need for marriage that there once was, but marriage is still important in society:

- It helps a couple to stay together because they have made a commitment to each other.
- It provides security for any children that might come along.

Making a go of it

These are the three basic things that couples will need to provide for each other when married, as well as money for recreation. Setting up a home of your own will take money and patience, in other words, a great deal of hard work! Some couples prefer to start off living with their parents. This has the advantage of being cheaper, and parents can help with cleaning, laundry and cooking when you both might be busy out at work earning money. If both of you work, it will be difficult to find the time and the energy to do household jobs properly. Living at home might also help you to save up to pay for a house deposit, or to have savings to fall back on for things like holidays, but there are disadvantages.

A newly married couple needs a great deal of privacy. You are starting a new life, and have much to discover about each other. You need to be free to make your own decisions, and free to argue if you feel like it. Living with parents might 'cramp your style' too much. They might interfere or you might not feel free to be yourself. This will put strain on a marriage.

You do not need to own your own property, of course. You could rent a flat or a council house. Finding the money for a mortgage, or for the rent, makes a couple pull together and work at their marriage. Privacy, freedom and challenges are essential ingredients in any marriage, especially at the beginning.

Who does what?

When you build a home together, how do you decide who does what? What roles do husbands and wives have?

Traditionally, the men went out to work and the women looked after the house. This arrangement stems from prehistoric times. The men hunted and took care of the animals; the women cultivated crops, made pottery and clothes, cooked, and reared the children. Some would argue that men are always physically stronger than women, and that is why this pattern developed. Others think, though, that women can train themselves to be as strong, but many women choose to rear their children since they came out of their bodies, and so there is a special link between them.

Many modern, Western couples both go out to work, letting a relative or a childminder look after their pre-school children for the working day. Most young couples see themselves as equal partners, sharing decisions. They have no set roles – the man might do house repairs in one family; the woman might do them in another, for example. It will differ from family to family.

Many Asian families are more traditional, with the husband and wife having set roles. The man might have more say outside the home, in his job and in business, but the wife will run the home and will be very influential there. She will decide on decoration, furniture, food and other details of housekeeping. She will be given great respect by the family for this. Their religions instruct the men to honour their wives for the work they do, and Hindus, for example, are supposed to model their relationships on that of the god Krishna and his partner Radha – a perfect example of the love a husband and wife should have for each other.

Religion and marriage

Religions value the marriage bond. Every religion has its own marriage ceremony. Religions tend to preserve and protect things in society that are thought to be good for civilisation. Marriage is preserved and blessed because it is a bond of commitment between two people, and it is a secure base for rearing children.

When a couple are brought before a priest, they are asking for God's help as they start off their married life. They acknowledge that God is their Lord, and that God has guided them together. They make their vows before God as well as before people, and the priest and the people pray for them. If you belong to a religious community and get married, then it feels as though there is a little extra help and support from the people who share your beliefs.

A marriage service is a time for rejoicing as two people start out on their new life together. There will usually be some kind of feast afterwards and the two different families are united in the act of eating, that most basic of human pastimes! Husbands and wives are seen to be God's gifts to each other, and their union is seen to be a special blessing. Some Christians refer to the union of a man and wife as a **sacrament**, an action which channels a blessing from God. Jews refer to marriage as a 'seal upon the heart'. The Muslim scriptures describe marriage in this way: 'He [God] has created wives for you . . . He has planted affection and mercy between you.' (Qur'an 30:21)

Non-religious people can marry in a register office, and this type of marriage is called **civil marriage**. For this, there has to be a person to conduct the marriage who is specially registered, and witnesses must be present. The couple make vows to each other in the presence of the witnesses.

A marriage is declared legal when the couple and the registrar or priest sign the marriage certificate. Christian and Jewish ministers can perform legal weddings, but in Britain members of other faiths have to be married in a register office as well.

HINDUISM

SIKHISM

JUDAISM

CHRISTIANITY

MUSLIM MARRIAGES ARE USUALLY ARRANGED. THE GROOM'S FAMILY IS EXPECTED TO GIVE A DOWRY — A GIFT OF MONEY OR HOUSEHOLD GOODS — TO THE BRIDE'S FAMILY. SHE WILL KEEP THIS AS A SECURITY IN CASE SHE IS EVER DIVORCED.

MUSLIM BRIDES FROM PAKISTAN OR INDIA WILL USUALLY DRESS IN RED SHALWAR AND KAMEEZ, AND WILL PAINT THEIR HANDS AND FEET. THEY WILL USUALLY SIT IN A SEPARATE ROOM FROM THE GROOM, IN HER HOME.

THE IMAM READS FROM THE FOURTH CHAPTER OF THE QURAN AND THEN GIVES A TALK ON THE DUTIES AND BLESSINGS OF MARRIAGE.

THE COUPLE ARE ASKED THREE TIMES IF THEY AGREE TO BE MARRIED, AND THEN THEY EXCHANGE RINGS. THE IMAM BLESSES THEM.

IN THE NAME OF ALLAH, THE COMPASSIONATE, THE MERCIFUL....

THE MARRIAGE CEREMONY ENDS WHEN THE COUPLE LEAD THE GUESTS TO A ROOM FOR CELEBRATION FEAST.

Divorce – marriages under strain

The Divorce Reform Act came into force on 1 January 1971. By this, a court of law could grant a divorce if a marriage could be shown to have broken down for any of the five reasons below:

1. If one partner has committed adultery.
2. If one partner has treated the other unreasonably (physical or mental cruelty, or if one partner is insane).
3. If one partner has been deserted by the other for a continuous period of two years.
4. If the partners have lived separately for two years, and both consent to a divorce.
5. If one partner does not consent to a divorce, then a divorce cannot be granted until they have lived apart for five years.

The 1984 Matrimonial and Family Proceedings Act now allows divorce after one year of marriage (rather than three years).

Every effort is made to make sure that the couple have tried to make their marriage work. This stops people from treating divorce and marriage too casually.

Marriages can come under stress, and couples often need someone to turn to for help and advice. There are many Marriage Guidance Counselling services that try to provide this, and they offer their services free of charge. Many couples can be helped to get over their problems, but some marriages do break down.

Most religions accept that some marriages do break down, although they encourage couples to do all they can to save their marriage first. Islam, for example, allows a man to divorce his wife, but Muslim tradition says that there is nothing more distasteful to God than divorce. Before a Muslim can divorce his wife, three things must have been done:

1. The man and wife must try to solve their problem.
2. If this does not work, then two friends or relatives give advice.
3. If this fails, then the couple must wait for four months before the marriage is ended.

Neither partner can remarry for a time after the divorce in case the woman finds that she is pregnant.

Most Christians accept divorce, but Roman Catholic Christians argue that a marriage can never be broken as the couple have been joined by God. They teach that marriage is a sacrament, and is binding for life. They take some words of Jesus as a basis for this:

'So they are no longer two, but one. Man must not separate, then, what God has joined together.' (Mark 10:8–9)

They also point out that St Paul does not allow divorce in his first letter to the Corinthian Christians, although he does allow couples to live separately. (I Corinthians 7:10–11) Roman Catholics do allow annulment, though. If a marriage is shown to have never taken place properly, it is cancelled (e.g. if one partner was insane or was forced into it against his/her will).

Other Christians point to the teaching of Jesus as recorded in Matthew 5:31–2. Here he allows divorce if a partner has committed adultery. If one thing can break the marriage bond, then might not other strains do so? They take the words in Mark 10:8–9 as the ideal, but admit that some marriages do break down.

Religions, then, say that marriage should be for life, and every effort should be made to work out this ideal, but some marriages might, sadly, break down beyond hope of repair.

Surviving a divorce

It is estimated that in Britain about one third of marriages end in divorce. A divorce is hard enough on the parents who have lived together for a number of years and have worked to raise a family. The children also suffer grief, anger, rejection and fear. People have to go through a grief process; they cannot just 'get over it' overnight. Over the page are the usual stages of the grief process:

Making arrangements . . .

Organise a class debate, with one team arguing for arranged marriages, and the other team arguing against.

What's it all in aid of?

1. Explain why marriages used to be like business deals in the past, and in some Third World countries today. Why has this changed in the West?
2. Write a short dialogue between two friends: one is trying to convince the other that there are still good reasons for getting married in the twentieth century.

Living together

Make a list of all the advantages and disadvantages that you can think of which are involved in living together without being married.

Playing the part!

1. Work out a role-play where a young married couple are living at home. The wife wants to have an argument about something, but the husband is afraid of upsetting his parents. What would they all say to each other?
2. Work out a role-play where a husband has chosen to stay at home and look after his child while his wife works. He meets some of his old friends and they start to tease him. What would they all say?
3. Work out a role-play as above, but this time the husband is a Muslim, Sikh or Hindu. What pressures would he be under then?

Till death us do part . . .

1. What are the main differences between a religious marriage ceremony and a civil one? How does a marriage ceremony help the couple to start off life together?
2. Read through the pages on various religious ceremonies, then list the ways in which they show concern for living a long life together, and for good fortune and children.
3. Write an account of a visit to a marriage service of any one religion, so long as it does not happen to be your own religion.
4. The Church of England marriage service gives three reasons why God wants people to be married. Compare the three reasons from the seventeenth-century service and the modern 1980 service:

   The 17th-century Book of Common Prayer
   a. So the couple can have children.
   b. So the couple will avoid the temptation of having sex outside marriage.
   c. So the couple can enjoy each other's company.

   The 1980 Alternative Service Book
   a. So the couple can enjoy each other's company.
   b. So the couple can enjoy sex with one another, marriage being the best place for sex.
   c. So the couple can have children if they want to.

   How does the modern service show that attitudes to sex and marriage have changed?

Broken hearts

1. The Law allows divorce for five reasons since 1971. What are these?
2. Think of three things that might cause stress in a marriage. How might a couple go about sorting these things out?
3. Do you think people should intend to get married for life?
4. What is the Muslim teaching on divorce?
5. Why do some Christians accept that some marriages should end in divorce while other Christians do not? (*Clue:* it's all about the traditions of what Jesus and St Paul taught about marriage.)

6 THE FAMILY

What type of family?

The traditional pattern of family life in the West is the **nuclear family**. Nuclear families are small in size, being restricted to mother and father and a few children. ('Nuclear' comes from the word *nucleus*, a basic group or arrangement.) However, many families today are **one-parent families** (about one in every eight). This is where one of the parents has to bring up the children on his or her own. This could be for a number of reasons, such as the death of a parent, but it is usually because of divorce, or because a woman becomes pregnant when unmarried and has to fend for herself. One-parent families tend to come under much more strain than nuclear ones for any or all of the following reasons:

- Not enough time: the parent has to earn money as well as bring up children, and this is very tiring and can be frustrating. There might not be enough time for recreation and talking together, or for following a hobby.

- Too much work: the parent has to be the breadwinner *and* the housekeeper – cooking and cleaning.
- Not enough money: there will only be one wage coming into the home, whereas there might have been two if a married couple was raising the children.

For these reasons, one-parent families are entitled to help from the Welfare State and from the social services.

In the past, most families had a large number of children, possibly as many as fourteen or fifteen! This was partly because living conditions were poorer, health care was worse, and many children died in infancy. Hence you had as many children as possible to make sure that you had heirs. Then it was their responsibility to look after you when you grew old. (Remember that this was before the old age pension.) Nowadays, some people in Britain choose to have large families, but most plan their families – restricting the number of children by the use of contraception. There is not the same need anymore to have large families.

Often grandparents, and possibly other relatives, would live with the family under the same roof. They all worked together to run the family and looked after one another. This kind of family is called an **extended family**. You can see that it is an *extension* of the basic unit – the nucleus of mother, father and children. Extended families either live under the same roof, or very close to each other. This was often the case in the old terraced streets of British towns and cities. A whole group of relations would be in one or two streets.

Muslims, Sikhs and Hindus usually follow the model of the extended family, and this forms

an important part of their religious beliefs. They try to follow this in the West as well. It is seen as a duty to God to look after elderly relatives, or any other relative who is going through hard times. As the Muslim holy book, the Qur'an, says:

> 'Show kindness to both your parents and to near relatives, orphans and the needy' (4:36) and one should 'give one's wealth away, no matter how one loves it, to near relatives.' (2:177)

Many Western people feel that the nuclear family is the best type of family because of the independence and freedom it gives. Of course, this freedom comes only because social conditions are better than in the past, but freedom might not be everything. Elderly people can feel lonely and ignored in our society because their children need not have any financial responsibility for them. This can lead to a carelessness, and they neglect to visit them. Members of Western families run the risk of feeling split up and removed from one another. Problems can also occur when a family has financial, health or marital difficulties. The family might find itself left on its own to cope, with little support from other relatives. This need not happen, of course, and many Western families maintain very close links with their relatives, but it is a danger in our system. People who live in an extended family might also argue that the children there grow up under the influence of more opinions and are used to dealing with people of different ages. These pros and cons have to be weighed up. Independence is very important, but perhaps not at the cost of cutting yourself off from the rest of your wider family. What do you think?

Israeli children on a kibbutz.

Alternatives to the family

Some people have tried to experiment with alternatives to the family. People live together in a group or a **commune**, sharing responsibilities. Men and women are equal, and children are looked after by other adults, as in a nursery. This releases the women for work. The idea is to teach people co-operation in an equal society.

Experiments with communes were tried in the Soviet Union to release women for work, but the family unit was just too strong and the idea was abandoned. Women still go out to work there, but nurseries are provided for their children.

China has had communes, but Chinese parents are encouraged to only have one child and they tend to look after it themselves. There have been various 'drop-out' communities in Western Europe and the USA, but these tend to be short-lived.

The most successful experiment with communes is the **kibbutz** system in Israel. Many of these were started in 1948, when the state of Israel was formed. Many of the Jewish people who emigrated there had suffered persecution in Europe because of Hitler, and they came full of ideals and determination to create a fairer society to live in. While the adults work, children are cared for in a nursery or in school. Schoolchildren have extra responsibilities, such as cleaning their own classrooms, to teach them tidiness and cleanliness. They also have to do some work on the farm, such as looking after the animals. They spend some time with their parents in the evenings and at the weekends, but they eat and sleep with their own age group.

Some Israelis have rejected the kibbutz system. They complain that it can make people too dependent on others, and takes away too much of your freedom. Some families prefer to join a farming co-operative where the work and profits are shared, but they live in their own homes.

Whatever valuable insights and skills children might learn from a commune, their own parents have a valuable role in their formation that should not be ignored.

Children

It is natural that children should make the closest relationships with their parents, especially in their early years. The child will share certain physical characteristics and certain emotional similarities with the parents, and it will develop a feeling of well-being and dependency from a very early age. When it is a baby, it feels hunger and cries, and a parent comes to feed it. The need is met, a feeling of well-being follows. The same applies if the child is frightened and then comforted. The parents are regular and consistent providers, and thus a deep relationship should be formed with them.

The life-style of a family will be changed when a new child comes along. Maybe the mother had been working before, and now she will be staying at home or only working part-time. This means that less money will be coming into the home. The daily routine will be different, someone having to be present to look after the baby's needs. This will take some getting used to, and while it might add some strain to the family at first, it should help the family to work together and bring them closer.

Socialisation occurs in the family; this is when a child learns how to cope with other people. This involves making demands and asking questions, learning respect for other people and learning how to cope with stressful relationships. The child learns from the parents and any brothers or sisters (or other relatives if in an extended family).

The family should provide three areas of care:

1. Physical care

2. Emotional care

3. Moral care

These three areas can be catered for by other relatives in an extended family or by sympathetic adults in a commune, but perhaps the most fruitful place to develop these might be with the child's own parents, because of the natural and deeper relationship that exists between them. This is something which the experts are still debating! Most adopted children grow up in a healthy and happy environment, for example. Their parents might not be their natural parents, but they are the closest adults who are committed to caring for them.

Everybody has a conscience, and this is partly formed by the socialisation process when you are a child. The famous saying, 'Give me the child for the first five years and he is mine for life,' is an extreme way of putting the same point. We are shaped by other people who we learn from, as children, and as we go through life. We are influenced by friends and people we respect. Yet we learn our basic values, our sense of right and wrong, from our parents. Hence, emotional and moral care is so important. (This is not to say that your conscience is *only* what you learnt from your parents – some values can be inherited, and seem to be part of the general memory of humankind, and some people would say that God can speak in your conscience, too.)

Everyone seems to have a basic awareness that if we hurt someone else then we are inviting them to hurt us. Our conscience leaps into action if ever we ignore this rule. Jesus once summed this up very well, 'Do for others what you want them to do for you.' (Matthew 7:12)

If a child is deprived of security, of emotional and moral care in its early years, then it might well find problems in relating to other people. It might become emotionally disturbed, depressed, or criminal. Our early years are so important.

71

Religion and the family

I have tried to show how basic and important the family is for the nurturing of children. Although other people can do a very good job up to a point, there is a natural link between members of a family that is special. Religions try to protect this and give great honour to the family. Parents are taught to be responsible and to care for their children by giving moral guidance. Children are taught to respect their parents in return. One of the Jewish commandments found in the Decalogue (The Ten Commandments) says:

> 'Respect your father and your mother, so that you may live a long time in the land I am giving you.' (Exodus 20:12)

This was written down centuries ago, when the Hebrews lived in extended families because there was no Welfare system. The idea was that if you took care of your responsibilities to your parents, then your children would learn from your example and look after you later on.

In one of the New Testament letters, parents and children are told to learn to respect one another:

> Children, it is your Christian duty to obey your parents . . . Parents, do not treat your children in such a way as to make them angry. (Ephesians 6:1–4)

Families of an Afro-Caribbean background in Britain tend to have a high regard for the family, with respect between children and parents. This is partly because of the strong Christian influence in many such families. Those who follow Rastafarianism will also have strong family ties. Asian parents are usually quite strict in raising their children since they take their religion's instructions to set a moral example seriously. White families will differ from home to home, but they do not tend to have strong moral guidelines like the Church used to provide – some will be strict, some not.

Happy families – Jewish style.

72

Making ends meet!

Write an imaginary letter to a newspaper as though you were a single parent. Outline all the problems and difficulties you have to face.

Stretching and shrinking!

1. What is the difference between a nuclear family and an extended family?
2. Why did most people have to live in extended families in Britain in the past?
3. List all the advantages and disadvantages of living in an extended family that you can think of.

All together now!

1. Why do you think that some people want to live in communes?
2. Why were many kibbutzim set up in Israel after World War Two?
3. If you had been brought up in a commune or a kibbutz, what do you think your life-style would have been as a young child? Do you think this would have had any benefits or disadvantages?
4. Why do you think that many people are opting out of the kibbutz system?
5. Why does a special relationship exist between parents and their children?

Care

1. Write a poem or short essay about the three types of care that parents should give to their children.
2. What do people think that conscience is based on?
3. Can you remember the first time you felt your conscience at work? Do you feel that this was because of something that your parents told you?
4. If a person grows up without any proper care as a child, how do you think he or she might be affected?

Respectfully yours . . .

1. One of the Ten Commandments says that children should respect their parents. Do you find it easy to respect them? If not, why do you think this is?
2. Do you think that respect has to be earned by adults, or can they just demand it from you? What has someone got to do to earn *your* respect, do you think?
3. Why do families with strong religious beliefs take the trouble to make their families work well? Do you have to be religious to have a strong family?

7 OLD AGE

Who is old?

When does a person start to be 'old' or 'elderly'? When you are a young child, a teenager seems grown-up, and someone in their twenties or thirties seems 'old'. When you are a teenager, anyone over 50 probably seems 'past it'! When you grow older, you think elderly people are much older – they must always be a good way ahead of you! Most adults tend to think that people start to be elderly when they retire and become pensioners. This is when men are 65 and women 60, though more people tend to take early retirement now, anywhere between 50 and 65 years of age. How do these retired people feel, themselves? Usually, people between 60 and 75 do not class themselves as being 'old', especially if their health is good and they have friends and are living a happy life. It is only when people reach the 80–90 age bracket that they might start feeling 'elderly', when their health fails and their memories are not as they were. There are exceptions, of course, and it all depends upon each person's feelings and state of health. The important thing to realise is that many people past the age of retirement do live happy lives, full of interests and hopes, even if they are not as active as when

they were younger. They are not necessarily 'past it'!

Many younger people, and society in general, do tend to think that elderly people have put the best years of their life behind them, and that they have to be kept comfortable until death takes them. This is a very sad attitude. Look at these typical remarks about the elderly from young people:

Those are the typical fears that young people have about old age. Yet, for many elderly people, these are not justified. For them it is a very different story. There are five things that elderly people can have that make their old age a happy one. These are freedom; interests; activities; reflection; and maturity.

Freedom

So long as a retired person is financially secure (having enough money from pensions and savings to pay bills) they will not have to work for a living any more. They will have time to themselves, to do the things they have always wanted to get around to doing. Younger people should really be jealous of this freedom!

Interests

Hobbies and interests can be indulged in and followed with all the free time a retired person has. There is no reason why a person should just 'switch off' the interests and concerns that have developed during their lifetime. They can carry on learning – and even take evening classes or other adult education courses just out of pure interest.

Activities

It is wrong to think that all old people are frail and incapable. Some are very fit and healthy for their age, and they can travel easily, take long walks or play simple sports. Many maintain an active sex life through their sixties and seventies, though it is generally true that companionship is the most important aspect of marriage at this age.

Reflection

Elderly people have more time to think about themselves and their lives. They can reflect upon all their experiences and try to find some point to their lives. If they are not as active, or are troubled by poor health, they compensate for this by their time to think. They are no longer rushed off their feet having to do things. This is another luxury they have that we should envy.

Maturity

In old age, people can gather together all their experiences and all their thoughts, and can come to terms with life. It is healthy for them to try to see their lives as worthwhile, even when things have made them suffer in the past. A wise person can see that something was learned and gained from the 'bad times'. If old people can come to terms with their lives in this way, and can come to terms with death, then they will have a calm attitude and a pleasant nature, and will not lose their friends.

This should present a much brighter picture than that imagined by many young people when they think of life after retirement on the Old Age Pension. These five things are not always present in the lives of old people, and problems then occur, but they often are present. Old age is only unhappy if people are troubled with poor health, if they have not got enough money, friends or hobbies, and if they cannot come to terms with themselves. Unhappy old people blame themselves for things they have done wrong in their lives, grow bitter about certain things that have happened and are scared of dying.

No use to society?

This attitude affects our society deeply, and many old people suffer to some extent because of it. It is the idea that if you are not working for a living, then you are not a valuable member of society, so you are to be shunted to one side and largely ignored. Some unemployed people feel that this is how they are treated as well as some elderly people. The danger is that this treats people like objects or machines – they are only good for what you can get out of them. It is like comparing a person to a can that contains a cold drink; once the drink has all gone, throw away the can. That is all it was made for, anyway. People are not like that, though. We have feelings and thoughts and we should be treated as though we are each special, special because we are alive, not for what we do. We should each be allowed to live out our lives as best we can, and be given the respect we deserve.

The elderly should therefore be given respect and enough resources to live out their lives as happily as possible, and, after all, they have worked hard and contributed to society in their younger days, anyway. They deserve a well-earned rest.

To enjoy their rest, and to have the freedom to pursue hobbies and to be fairly comfortable, elderly people have to be financially secure. The state pension in 1986 for a single person was £38.30 and it was £61.30 for a married couple. This is only a modest weekly income to live off in twentieth-century Britain. Many retired people also receive a work's pension from their old employers and this supplements the weekly income to a reasonable level.

The state pension was first introduced in 1908 with the Old Age Pensions Act, and this gave people over seventy 25p a week if they were earning less than 50p per week! It has been increased many times over since then, and the age lowered to sixty-five. Still, Britain's expenditure on pensions is about in the middle of the European league table. West Germany provides the highest figures, closely followed by the Netherlands. Trade Unions campaign for more frequent increases to match the cost of living; they suggest reviews every six months, and extra help during the winter months to cover fuel bills.

It is true that many pensioners own their own homes (though

some have to rent them from the Council or from private landlords), but they still need money for rates, heating and repairs. They need enough money to eat properly if they are to maintain their good health, and they will need money for recreation – which is how they will spend most of their time – following hobbies, reading, studying, travelling or going on outings and trips to the theatre or cinema. Clearly, if they do not get enough money, then the quality of their lives will suffer and their morale will deteriorate.

Pensions are financed by the National Insurance Scheme. A working person pays a contribution to the state, and pensions are paid out of this money when they retire. If people have no work's pension, they can apply for a supplementary pension that will increase their state pension.

The generation gap

Elderly people tend to feel more ignored today in the West than they did in the past because of the 'generation gap'. In the past, the pace of life was much slower. There were fewer inventions, and the style of life changed very little from one generation to the next. This meant that elderly people were more respected and honoured in society. They had lived longer, and so were more experienced in the ways of the world. They were regarded as the wise citizens. The elders of a town or a village felt they were much more the focus of attention than do most elderly people today who have mainly withdrawn from society to enjoy their retirement.

In various parts of the world, the West in particular, the pace and style of life is always changing as technology introduces new invention after new invention. Think of the different things that have been introduced since the turn of the century – aircraft, space rockets, television, computers, the silicon chip . . . not to mention time-saving devices for the kitchen such as dishwashers and microwave ovens! The way an elderly person was brought up was different from the way you have been brought up, surrounded by many things you take for granted. For this reason, elderly people are not looked up to as experienced and wise in our society. They are thought to be 'behind the times'. It is true that the new technologies do baffle many elderly people (though not all), and so they cannot be turned to for any sort of technical wisdom, but they are still more experienced in emotional areas of life and can be of great help to younger relatives or friends when they go through suffering and tragedy. They can give understanding and encouragement because they have been through similar things.

Besides this, it is no crime to withdraw from the technical side of society and to enjoy a well-earned rest. Western young people need to learn a new respect for the elderly, although it is true that the old basis of respect cannot be revived.

Three generations who live (and work) together.

Asian families of Hindus, Sikhs and Muslims in the West are careful to maintain their custom of treating the elderly with great respect. Many live in extended families, of course, looking after their aged relatives at home, and listening to their advice and giving them a degree of authority in the home. Asians fear that Western society neglects the elderly too much, and even when the state will provide for them, they feel that it is also their duty to provide for them as their kin. It is a way of repaying them for the time and attention the parents spent on them when they were children. The scriptures of these faiths demand this duty to parents. The Muslim holy book, the Qur'an, says this (17:23–5):

> Show kindness to your parents; whether either or both of them attain old age [while they are] still with you, never say to them: 'Ough!' nor scold either of them . . . Serve them with tenderness and humility and say: 'My Lord show them mercy, just as they cared for me as a little child.'

Christians and Jews try to give respect to the elderly, but there is no strong sense of duty to look after them in the family's own home, although individual families might choose to do this. Jewish rabbis and Christian ministers will visit the homes of elderly members of their congregations, and special services, meals, outings and social clubs will be arranged by synagogues and churches.

In Western society, families tend to be wary about letting elderly relatives live with them. They fear that this would mean less freedom for everybody concerned. The elderly person might feel limited: he or she has to fit in with the routine of the family. Elderly people might feel too dependent upon the family, when retirement ought to give them the opportunity of running their own lives and of being free.

There might be clashes between grandchildren and grandparent or elderly relative. Their attitudes to many things in life – religion, politics, fashion, music – might be very different, with neither side understanding the other. When they live separately, it is easier to be tolerant, but when you are all under the same roof, the strain begins to show!

The parents might not feel sure of how to treat their elderly parents, perhaps treating them more like children since they have become dependent upon them. The problems here are caused by the different upbringing Western people have to that of Asian or Eastern people. They are taught to value independence much more, and do not have the same strong religious values. Thus it is very hard to adapt from a nuclear family to an extended one; it creates many tensions.

Of course, many old people are able to live alone in our society, so long as their health is good. They have state welfare, and so they can usually be financially independent. Difficulties occur when their health fails, and they cannot look after themselves any more.

If elderly people do not go to live with their families, there are three possibilities:

Home help

If their health is good enough, the social services can provide a daily helper to come in for a short time, to help with shopping cooking and cleaning.

Sheltered accommodation

This is where an elderly person is given their own flat within a hostel or group of flats that has a warden. If they get into any difficulties – such as falling, and they are unable to pick themselves up, then they ring for the warden to come and help. Some of these hostels have their own laundries, recreation rooms and dining-rooms, where people can go if they wish, to mix with the other residents. Sheltered accommodation thus gives elderly people a measure of independence and freedom.

Old people's homes

Here, an elderly person will usually have less privacy as so many facilities are shared with others. Some seem very happy in such places, but others react strongly against institutional living, and feel too dependent. There is little that can be done about this if the person's health has deteriorated.

It might be very difficult for Western families to look after their elderly relatives, but if society paid more respect to the elderly, and young people were brought up to think of them as people who were living out their lives, and not just as people who were 'past it', perhaps more thought would be given to elderly relatives living alone. If the family cannot take them in, they do need to visit them regularly and pay attention to them, to make them feel that they are still wanted.

Euthanasia

Euthanasia means, literally, 'a good death'. It means letting people die who are suffering great pain, rather than keeping them alive at all costs. It is sometimes referred to as 'dying with dignity'. In our modern age we have the technology and medical knowledge to keep many people alive who would have died of their illnesses in times past. Some people argue that very old and ill people should be able to choose to die. Doctors would then stop keeping them alive by artificial means, and the patient would die peacefully.

The Voluntary Euthanasia Society was formed by Lord Moynihan, a former member of the Royal College of Surgeons, in 1935. (It used to be known as EXIT.) It campaigns for the right to die with dignity. Rather than be kept alive when there is little or no hope of a cure, and having to suffer great pain, they say you should be able to choose to die. They want careful safeguards, though, and do not want to simply encourage suicide. By their proposed system, people would have to sign a declaration at least 30 days before their request for euthanasia, and this must be independently witnessed by two people, unrelated to the patient, and who do not stand to benefit from the patient's death. Two doctors would then have to testify that the patient was in great pain with little hope of recovery.

Some people fear that if voluntary euthanasia were allowed, then it would make it easier for people in the future to abuse the idea. Then, anyone who was a burden to society – the old, the disabled, the mentally ill, for example, could be quietly killed off, under the name of 'mercy killing'. Nazi Germany, under Hitler, had a programme of compulsory euthanasia for certain types of people. This was to defend the 'Master Race', as they called themselves, from any weakness or impurity. The Society does not want anything like the horrible

system of compulsory euthanasia, but some think that if any form of euthanasia is allowed, then it would be the 'thin end of the wedge', and governments in future might relax the laws that would carefully limit it. Others argue that if voluntary euthanasia were to be introduced, then pressure might be put upon a sick, elderly relative to choose this option. The pressure might come from relatives or even from hospital staff who might be working in stressful and overcrowded conditions.

Religious people also have different opinions about euthanasia. Most Asian religions would be opposed to it because of their strong sense of duty to look after elderly relatives, and because they feel that life is special, and that only God should decide when a person dies, unless it is in the case of the punishment of a criminal or in a war.

Some Jews and Christians also oppose voluntary euthanasia. They think that life is sacred and should be preserved at all costs. Roman Catholic Christians strongly oppose it, stressing that it might undermine respect for innocent human life. It might encourage society to think that elderly people were a burden to be disposed off. They fear that voluntary euthanasia could lead to worse forms of euthanasia being practised later on.

Other Jews and Christians argue for voluntary euthanasia. Life might be special and sacred, but what if all the dignity, beauty and meaning in a life has vanished? (i.e. If people are very old, frail and going through extreme suffering, or if they are totally paralysed with no hope of recovery, or in a coma being barely kept alive on life-support machines.) These people stress that death is not the end of life, but the doorway into a joyful new life with God, and so release from pain might be merciful and not evil, so long as careful safeguards are kept.

Religion and old age

Many elderly people start to think about religion more than they did in their youth; they are drawing to the close of their lives and are trying to come to terms with death. It is natural to think more about religious beliefs at this time, and to wonder about what might happen after death. For those with a religious faith, it is a time of preparing to go back to God, and to be released from this life.

The Hindu religion makes special provision for this stage in life. The Hindu's life is divided into four stages, or *ashramas*. These are supposed to last for 25 years each. The first is concerned with education and learning a trade; the second is concerned with raising a family and running a home; but the third and fourth stages are very different. The third stage is supposed to begin when a person is 50. Then, the man and wife will retire from their work, and withdraw to a simple dwelling, often in the forest. Their wealth is given away, and they learn to abandon the various pleasures of life. When the man is about 75, he is supposed to leave his wife and live as a wandering holy man, begging for food, praying and meditating, and teaching people. He renounces the world completely, and when he makes this decision, other elderly holy men will hold a mock funeral for him, burning a small effigy of the man. This is to stress that he is dead to the world. Not many Hindus choose to follow these final two stages in life because it demands too much of them, but that is what their scriptures recommend. By taking these steps, a Hindu man tries to prepare himself for his return to God.

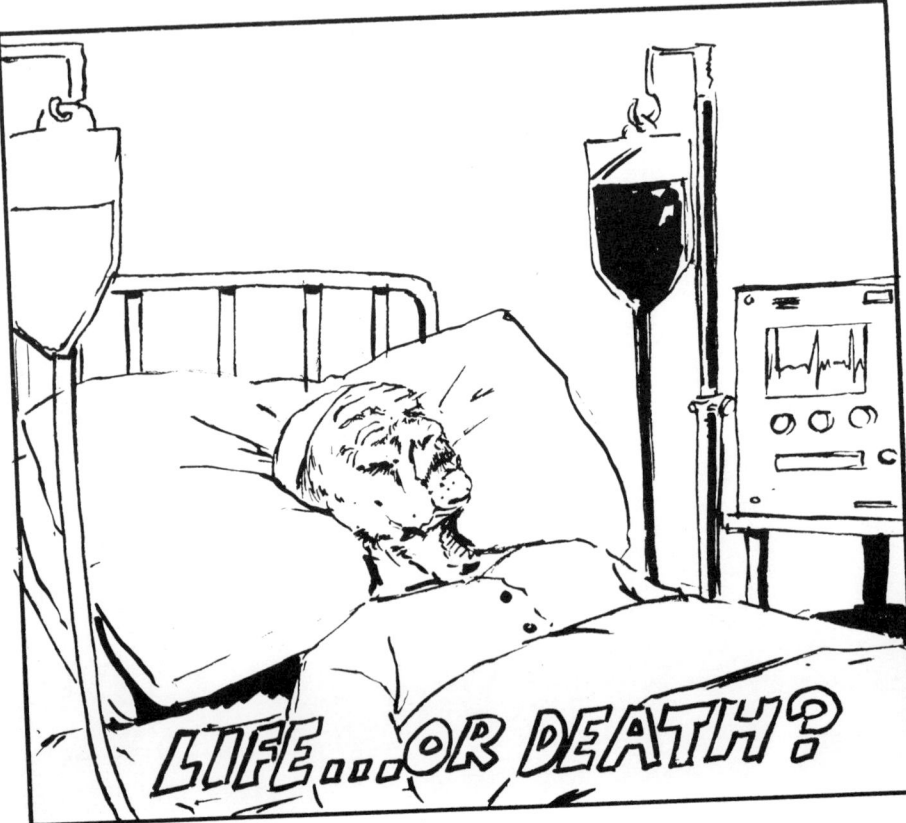
LIFE...OR DEATH?

A Hindu holy man in the final stage of life.

To sum up then:

Elderly people are not all incapable!

Many stay healthy and active for some time!

Elderly people deserve a rest!

They have worked hard in their lives, and now they have a right to more time and freedom of their own.

Elderly people deserve respect!

They are people with their own feelings and ideas just as you have!

Elderly people deserve adequate provision!

They should have enough money, good health care, housing and recreational facilities so that they can live out their lives in peace and comfort.

81

What do you expect?

1. Hold a class discussion on people's attitudes to old age. Then, list your own attitudes.
2. Read through pages 75-6 and compare these ideas with your list of what you expect old age to be like. Does anything surprise you? Has this made you think again?
3. Write a short dialogue between a young grandson and his grandfather. Have the grandfather trying to convince the grandson that life for him is not boring. Stress how he makes up for not being as active.

Generation gap

1. Why do many young people in the West today find that there is a generation gap between them and the elderly? Talk or write about a personal experience that you have had of this.
2. What help and advice are elderly people still able to give in Western society?
3. How do you think young people can try to break down the generation gap? Suggest some practical things to do.

On the pension

1. When were old age pensions first introduced? How much were they then?
2. Do you think the pension is enough to live on now? Work out what you think old people will need to live a happy life.
3. What ways are there of getting extra money if the pension is not enough?
4. How would you answer someone who said that old people should not be looked after because they cannot work any more?

Home sweet home?

1. What would be the advantages and disadvantages of living with your family when you are elderly?
2. Write a short essay where you are an old person living in your daughter's home, with her family. Set this in any part of the day, having some other members of the family present, and choose an incident or situation that brings out some of the advantages or disadvantages mentioned above.
3. How do many Asian families look after their elderly relatives? Why do you think that they find this easier than many Western families?
4. What is meant by sheltered accommodation? What other two options are there for elderly people who do not live with their families?

Approaching journey's end . . .

1. What is meant by 'euthanasia'? List some arguments for and against it.
2. Do you think that you would want to be kept alive when you were very old and in pain? If you agree with euthanasia, what safeguards would you want introduced?
3. Why do you think that some people become more religious when they are elderly?
4. How does the Hindu religion try to help elderly men to cope with the arrival of death?
5. Write a few paragraphs imagining that you are an old Hindu man who is starting to follow the final stage of life. How do you think you would feel?

8 DEATH... AND BEYOND?

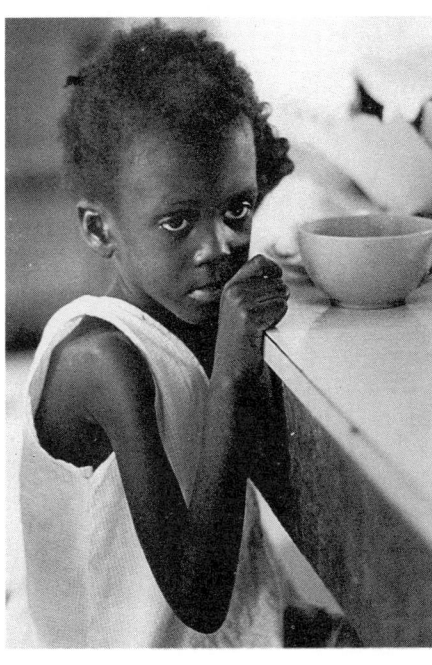

minds, thinking that we've got a long life to live yet. That it should not be something to concern us.

We are cushioned and protected by the technological achievements of our society. The death of an old person is 'messy' and unpleasant, but this can be lived with. However, if a tragedy occurs, if a younger person dies in an accident or from a disease, then we are devastated. We do not know how to cope with the feelings, the pain, the anger, the emptiness. Western people have lost the ability to face up to death, to live with it. Earlier generations knew how to cope, how to console one another.

Every living thing has to die; nothing in nature lasts for ever. Everything has a beginning, and everything has an end. Life is *finite*, limited. The human life-span has increased in the West, and in parts of the East, with new technologies that cure diseases, replace damaged organs and bring a prosperous life-style that allows most people to eat well.

This is not the case all over the world, though. Many Third World countries are poverty stricken. There are large numbers of unemployed, or many people have to work hard for very little money. If there is little money, then investments cannot be made to develop agriculture, and if there is too much rain or too little rain one year, a famine will result. Hundreds if not thousands of people will lose their lives. Even when there is no famine, young children will be undernourished, and will be more prone to disease. A Third World family will probably be far more used to death than will a Western family. Western people knew far more about death in previous centuries, though. There were famines and epidemics of disease here, and the working classes suffered greatly. People had large families to ensure that some of their children survived into adulthood.

People in the West do not like to speak about death. It frightens us and we are not sure of how we should cope with it. The Victorians did not like to talk about sex, but we do not want to talk about death! It is almost like a forbidden subject. We encounter it only on rare occasions; usually with the death of an elderly relative. Then we can push it to the back of our

83

Coping with death

The Third World might offer a harsher life style, but it also shows our culture up. It offers customs and values that help people when they are faced with the death of a relative or a friend. Some people in rural African villages teach the children how to help a bereaved person. They start when they are very young, the equivalent of the Infant School years here. The adult provides a doll, and a girl has to act the part of the mother weeping for her lost 'baby'. The other children gather round her to weep with her. They all touch her, hold her, comfort her, as the doll is buried in the ground. This lesson prepares them for the real thing. It helps them to face up to death, and to release the right emotions.

By contrast, most Western people feel emotionally 'bottled up' when faced with death. We are embarrassed and unsure of our feelings. We tend to be reserved when meeting the bereaved person. We might be silent in their presence or, even worse, we will probably try to talk about anything *but* the death, getting them to keep going as though nothing has happened.

The people who seem to know how to cope with bereavement best in Britain today are usually the elderly, or people from a strong religious or cultural tradition. The elderly were brought up when British society was very different. When a family was mourning the death of a relative, the whole street would join in. People might wear black, or black armbands, and the neighbours would rally round in support in a variety of ways – visiting, talking, weeping, giving gifts, or whatever. More importantly, though, it would be as if a hush had settled on that community for a time. People stopped and thought; life did not just speed on around the bereaved as usual.

Down the street thirty years ago.

This has all changed with the faster pace of life, the high-rise flats, and the new estates where there is not the same sense of community. This sense of community does exist, though, among Afro-Caribbeans, or among Asians or among Jews. These people have strong family ties, cultural traditions and, often, deeply religious beliefs. Afro-Caribbeans will show emotion openly, and a funeral will be crowded at a church. Hindus will rally round one another. (In India, in fact, an entire village would attend a funeral.)

Jews have a custom called **shiva** where people will visit mourners at their home for seven days. Time is to be set aside to this; it is an obligation, a responsibility to your friends or relatives. The bereaved might

sometimes feel that they would prefer to be alone, but the rabbi will encourage them to receive visitors. They will feel supported; they will be able to express their emotions, and all this will help them to carry on with life. Note that they are encouraged to express their feelings; it is not healthy to repress or 'bottle up' how you feel. In fact, when many Jewish people hear of the death of a friend or of a relative, they will tear the collar or lapel of the garment they are wearing. This helps them to let out their feelings.

For anyone, of any race, the bereavement process lasts for about eighteen months to two years. This is the amount of time needed to adjust to life without the friend or relative who was very close to you. It is not something that people can just snap out of. The bereavement process will be hindered if a person is not able to express their grief. Tears, and shouts, can be healing.

Funerals

A funeral is a way of showing some last respect for the deceased person. Family and friends gather together to say a last 'goodbye' to their friend or relative. Different races and cultures have customs for preparing the body for burial or for cremation. The body will be washed clean. Hindus rub sandalwood paste on to the forehead of the corpse, Sikhs wash the body with yoghurt and water, and Muslims perform a ritual of the body that begins with the **wuzu** (the washing of face, hands and feet before Muslims perform their daily prayers) and finishes with a total washing.

A deceased person's body may be clothed in something very simple like a white robe, or something much more elaborate. Sikhs dress the corpse up in a new suit of clothes, including shoes. Jewish men are buried with their prayer shawls wrapped round their shoulders. This is a way of showing respect as they are sent out of this life.

In the West, most people wear black at a funeral. This suggests sorrow. Bright, colourful clothes would suggest life and joy, and these are not appropriate. Some other cultures wear white, as in India, or as in China, to suggest mourning.

The gathering, the gifts, the tears and the prayers at a funeral are all a way of saying, 'Thanks for the memory' of the deceased person.

An afterlife?

'Everything that lives has to die. But why?' That is a question that many, many people ask themselves. One of the reasons why we have to die one day is so that we can make room for others on the earth. In other words, if no one died, the world would be overcrowded! A generation passes away; a new generation is born.

Another reason for dying is that our bodies wear out. We grow old, and are not able to do many of the things we used to. People grow tired after seeing and doing many things if they have lived a long life. Death is like a peace, a release, a rest.

Is that all, though? Is death the end of the line? Does life's journey really stop there and go no further? If so, then what has it all been for? What has been the point of all the fuss and bother, the laughter and the hopes? Furthermore, what about young people who die 'before their time'? Is that it for them?

Most people throughout history have believed that death is not the end of the line. The journey continues, somehow, after death, in a new life. Death is like a door that opens on to a new life, a new stage, a new journey. Perhaps death is like sleep. We sleep to break up and sort out all of the day's experiences, and to give our bodies a rest. Perhaps we die to finish one life, to have a rest, and to move on to another.

Many people in the world do still believe in an afterlife, especially if they are religious, but more people are doubting this than ever before, particularly in the West, and in Communist countries. Here, many find it too hard to believe in, or find it all very confusing. This means that some people are growing up thinking that death is the end, that there is nothing after it.

'May the Force be with you!'

If people think death is the end, then they do not like to talk about it. We tend to be cushioned against death by the technology in our society; we do not have to live with death every day, and there is a widespread attitude that there is nothing else after death, 'Once you're dead, you're dead!'

This is because countries with scientific and technological knowledge are used to dealing with things that can be touched and seen and measured. They are not used to dealing with invisible things like spiritual matters – God, the soul, a spirit world, other dimensions . . . Religion deals with these things, and while religion still plays a significant part in the world, it is not as widespread or as influential as it once was.

While many people would say they were doubtful about a life after death, they are fascinated by science fiction films and stories about hyperspace and parallel universes, or by role-playing fantasy games with magic spells and an afterlife for the boardgame heroes! People do not like to think that we are all alone in this universe; there must be something else. If people do not turn to religion, they usually turn to a substitute – a game, a film, a fantasy story, to express their dreams and hopes.

Science has not proved that there is no such thing as an afterlife, though. Scientific knowledge is limited to this physical universe. If there is anything beyond this physical universe, then science simply cannot investigate it. That does not mean that there is nothing else; it means that you cannot prove that there is. You are quite free to believe that there is a life after death if you want to, and there are many intelligent people who do believe in one, but you're just following a 'hunch', not proof.

Early beliefs

The earliest evidence of a belief in an afterlife comes from the age of Neanderthal Man. The Neanderthals lived between about 100,000 to 40,000 years ago. They buried their dead with their belongings – tools and weapons mainly. The bodies were curled up in the position of a new-born baby, perhaps suggesting that the dead person was about to be reborn into a new life. A grave at Shanidar in Iraq had had flowers scattered around and over the body.

Many ancient cultures buried objects with the dead person, and the most elaborate system was in Egypt. The bodies of the dead were preserved. Poor people were sometimes just covered in a layer of bitumen to keep out the air, but richer people were mummified. This meant that their internal organs were removed, and their bodies were wrapped in yards of linen bandage. These mummies were placed in elaborate tombs with their personal possessions, such as in the pyramids. The idea was that the souls of the dead could use their belongings in the next life. Ancient Egyptians believed that the soul went on a journey to the Underworld where they were judged by a god called Osiris.

In the tomb of Tutankhamun.

The idea that a dead person's soul needs its earthly posessions in the next life seems childish. These were very early ways of believing in a life after death. Later it became clearer that 'you can't take it with you', to use the popular expression. The spirit or soul left everything behind in this world and moved on.

Reincarnation

One belief, called **reincarnation**, was developed in India, and is now taught by Hindus, Buddhists and Sikhs. It has also become very popular in the West. Reincarnation means that a dead person's soul is reborn on earth, either as a human or as an animal. The soul is immortal, and is part of God. God is the Spirit behind all life, and the soul is like God's breath, or like a spark from a fire. Most people forget that they have come from God, and they become distracted by earthly pleasures. They must live many lives until they seek God and remember that they are part of God. Life is then like a series of journeys until the soul is ready to rejoin with God. Hindus call this reunion **moksha**, and Sikhs call it **mukti**, words which mean 'release' or 'freedom' from being reborn on earth. Buddhists do

Stillness . . . a Buddhist monk meditating.

not believe in a God, but in a force of life that we must all return to. For a Buddhist, when a person 'wakes up' to their need to live a holy life and to escape being reborn, this is 'enlightenment' and the soul is ready to enter the condition of 'Nirvana'. This means to be 'cooled' of all desires and to enter perfect peace.

Death, then, for a Hindu, Buddhist or Sikh, is the end of one life and the start of another. All their lives are a journey or pilgrimage to the point where they are ready to join the mysterious reality called God, or the Life Force.

The union with the One Spirit is compared to a drop of water returning to the ocean. The ultimate hope, then, is not to live in a heaven, but to actually share in the divine life, to be absorbed into God. If a person asks what this will be like, or asks if they will have any identity of their own when living-in-God, a spiritual teacher of one of those religions would reply, 'It is beyond words; beyond knowledge; beyond description. It is impossible to know what it will be like. All that can be said is that it will be perfect peace and bliss.' It is like asking an ant what it would be like to live as a human being!

The soul's progress depends on the good and bad deeds it stores up. This store, or record, is called **karma**. If a person lives an evil life, then they will either be born very poor, or go through much suffering in their next life, or even be born as an animal. If this bad karma is cancelled out by good deeds, then the soul will progress. Hindus and Buddhists believe in serving their fellow men, and giving up time to meditate and study their scriptures to cancel out bad karma. Sikhs stress that God will forgive or cancel out bad karma if a person opens his or her life to God in prayer, praise and service. A holy Sikh is called **gurmukh**, 'God-filled'. Their scriptures say, 'If God abides with you undisturbed, you will not be reborn.'

The soul is indestructible, and will journey on until it reaches its goal.

> As a man leaves an old garment and puts on one that is new, the Spirit leaves his mortal body and then puts on one that is new. (The Gita 2:22)

Sikhs filled with God; filled with joy!

89

Judaism

The Jews developed a different idea of the afterlife. At first, they believed in a shadowy 'ghostland' called Sheol that was under the ground, and everybody went there. Good people were thought to live a long, happy life on earth, and evil people were supposed to suffer. In time, it became clear that this was often far from true! Evil people often grew rich and lived a long time in luxury, while a good man might be poor. It also dawned on them that God must have something greater than a life in 'ghostland' for them.

Eventually, the belief in resurrection emerged. This teaches that God will give a person a new life after death; they will be 'raised up'. They will not be a ghost – they will be fully alive, but in a new way. The Book of Daniel in the Hebrew Bible was the first to spell out this belief. (The Hebrew Bible is what Christians call the Old Testament.)

> 'Many of those who have already died will live again: some will enjoy eternal life, and some will suffer eternal disgrace. The wise leaders will shine with all the brightness of the sky.' (Daniel 12:2–3)

Jews call this new life 'Olam Ha'ba', 'the World to Come'. Some think this is in another universe or dimension. Others think this is on this earth in the future, when it has been transformed.

Sinful people are punished in some way; they will not get away with their evil deeds for ever, even if they seemed to do so in their earthly life! Most Jews believe that after some suffering these souls are purified, and then they can enter Olam Ha'ba. Righteous souls go there straight away. Jews also say that it is impossible to know exactly what it will be like to live again in the resurrection; it is beyond human knowledge. It is enough to know that it will be perfect peace and joy.

One of the prayers at a Jewish funeral goes like this:

> He makes death to vanish in life eternal; and the Lord God wipes away tears off all faces.

Jews are never cremated because they feel this would be dishonouring their bodies which God will one day raise up.

Christianity

Christians also believe in resurrection. They inherited this idea from Judaism, and see a proof of it in the story of the resurrection of Jesus. The first disciples of Jesus said that they saw appearances of the risen Christ after his crucifixion. He had been placed in a tomb, and on the morning of the third day after, the mysterious power of God raised him up. The body disappeared from the tomb, and the disciples saw visions of Jesus and talked with him on and off over a period of about 40 days. There are several versions of these appearances at the end of each of the four Gospels in the New Testament, for example:

> It was late that Sunday evening, and the disciples were gathered together behind locked doors, because they were afraid of the Jewish authorities. Then Jesus came and stood among them. 'Peace be with you . . . As the Father sent me, so I send you.' (John 20:19–21)

Christians do not think that Jesus was just a dead man walking again, like someone who dies briefly and then revives. They believe that Jesus had been raised up; transformed! In the Gospel stories of the resurrection, he sometimes shines with light, or he suddenly appears in locked rooms, or he looks different, so that his disciples do not recognise him at first. Christians believe that he had become something much greater, and that he lives on today. They say that he lives in God, and is one with God.

This belief gives comfort to Christians at the funeral of a dead friend or relative. Hopefully they will share in the resurrection. According to John's Gospel, Jesus said, 'I will raise them to life on the last day.' (6:40)

Christians also believe in 'the World to Come', like the Jews, but they usually call it 'Heaven'. Contrary to popular belief, this is not supposed to be a place in the sky, somewhere. It is something spiritual, in another dimension. It is not supposed to be something physical, and therefore it cannot be located anywhere in space or time.

In the ancient world and in medieval times, when people did not understand much about science and the structure of the universe, the more uneducated people thought that heaven was up above the clouds – they did not know that space was up there, and the clouds seemed to be hiding something mysterious.

They also thought that Hell was under the earth, and that was where all the evil people went, and it was full of fire and devils. (Partly because the dead were buried under the ground, and volcanoes sent flames shooting up from below.)

Out of the mouth of Hell! A performance by the Medieval Players.

The risen Christ appeared to the disciples.

This was popular superstition, though. 'The World to Come' was going to be something new and spiritual, not floating around in the sky somewhere! In the New Testament, Jesus promises that it will happen, but he does not try to describe how or where. It is to be a surprise and a mystery. Christians do believe that people will be judged for the evil they have done, but very few now believe that sinners will be thrown into a fiery place. Perhaps Hell is a state of being cut off from God and God's blessings; perhaps the flames are symbolic of being purified, of evil being 'burned up' and destroyed. Some Christians think that Hell lasts for ever, while others think that it is temporary, to teach people a lesson and to purify them. Some Anglican, Roman Catholic and Orthodox Christians believe in Purgatory, and in-between place between Hell and Heaven, where people who are not very evil can be prepared for Heaven. Most Christians now stress that God is love and that God will not easily give up on people.

Islam

Muslims believe in resurrection, as well as Jews and Christians. The Prophet Muhammad stressed that life after death came only by the power of God. God was the Creator of the world, so could God not also raise the dead to new life? Many Arabs of Muhammad's day seemed to have mocked him for teaching this, and there are many examples of verses like this in the Qur'an:

> Does not man think We shall never put his bones together again? Indeed, We can remould his very fingers!

The resurrection will happen at the Day of Judgement, when the true believers will enter Paradise and the unbelievers will enter Hell.

> On that day there shall be joyous faces, looking towards their Lord. On that day there shall be mournful faces, dreading some great affliction.

Paradise and Hell are described in very physical terms. Paradise is like a garden of delights, with cool streams and rivers of milk and honey. In Hell, people will drink scalding water that will rip into their bowels! Some Muslims take this word for word. They think that God has actually prepared two places like that in some other dimension or parallel universe. Other Muslims take these descriptions as picture-language, as symbols. Paradise is perfect bliss, and Hell is torment and suffering, and the descriptions in the Qur'an are just ways of getting these ideas across.

Many Muslims think Hell will last for ever, but others think it is temporary, a place where people will be punished and purified so that they will turn from their sins.

Muslims are never cremated; they are always buried. This is because of their belief in a physical resurrection of some kind. They are buried with their heads facing Mecca, their holy city.

Prayers at a mosque in Walsall.

Life after death is a belief; it cannot be proved. Many people believe in it because they think there must be more than just this world. Some try to find proof that you survive the death of your body, though. Here are a few examples.

Out-of-the-body experiences

Some people claim to have felt their souls leave their bodies for a short time. They say they could look down on their bodies below. This is usually reported after an accident, when the person can remember seeing all the people who gathered round to help them, even though they were unconscious at the time. For example, one man was at the front of a coach when it crashed. When he was unconscious, he kept on thinking, 'Who will help the child trapped under the back wheel? They won't see him from the front here!' When he came to, some men were carrying the child to safety. How did he know there was a child under the back wheel of the coach?

Ghosts

Ghost stories are always popular. Many are made up, but some might be true. A recent ghost sighting took place in the seventies in Manchester on a double-decker bus! A man got on at a stop and went upstairs. He was the only passenger upstairs, and when the conductor went up to collect his fare, there was no one there! No one had seen him get off and the bus had not stopped! Later, the driver and conductor found out that their bus followed the route of an old tram. At the end of the war, a soldier returned home only to find that his wife had left home and was living with someone

INDEX

abortion, 50
Abraham, 21, 23
afterlife, 87–93
alcohol, 13, 31, 32, 34
Allah, *see* God
Amrit, 20, 34, 36
annulment, 65
Aqeeqah, 18, 23
archarya, 35
arti flame, 60
ashramas, 80
Aum, 19

baptism, 18, 22, 38
   believer's baptism, 38
Bar Mitzvah, 34, 37
Bat Mitzvah, 34, 37
bereavement, 84–6
Bible, the, 10, 37, 53, 65, 71, 72, 90–1
Big Bang, the, 7, 9, 10
birth, 16–24
Brit Milah, 21
Buddhism/Buddhists, 89

Call to Prayer, the, 23
candles, 22
Christening, 22
Christianity/Christians, 13, 18, 22, 34, 38, 50, 51, 53, 59, 63, 65, 72, 78, 80, 90–1
chupah, 62
churches, 22, 78
circumcision, 18, 21, 23
communes, 70, 71
conception, 16, 17
Confirmation, 34, 38
contraception, 47–8, 51, 56, 69
covenant, 21, 23
creation myths, 9–10
cremation, 90, 92
cross, sign of the, 22

Day of Judgement, 92
death, 76, 93–4; *see also* euthanasia
divorce, 55, 64, 65–6, 68

Divorce Reform Act, 65
dowries, 56, 64
drinking, *see* alcohol

Earth, the, 7, 8, 9
Egyptians, Ancient, 88
euthanasia, 79

family, the, 68–73
   extended, 69, 71, 78
   nuclear, 68, 69, 78
   one-parent, 68–9
foetus, development of the, 16, 50
friends, 29, 31, 32, 44, 76
funerals, 87

Gay Liberation Movement, 53
generation gap, 77–8
ghosts, 90, 92–3
Gobind Singh, Guru, 36
God, 9–10, 12, 13, 18, 19, 20, 21, 23, 34, 35, 36, 39, 53, 59, 65, 69, 71, 80, 88, 89, 90, 91, 92
godparents, 22
Granth, the, 20, 61
Granthi, 20
growing up, 25–40
gurdwaras, 20, 36
gurmukh, 89

Heaven, 91
Hebrew, 37
Hell, 91, 92
heroes, 30
Hinduism/Hindus, 18, 19, 34, 35, 51, 55, 58, 60, 69, 78, 80, *81*, 85, 87, 89
Holy Spirit, 38
home help, 79
homo habilis, 8
homo sapiens sapiens, 8–9
homosexuality, 52–3
hormones, 26, 47, 53

Islam/Muslims, 13, 18, 23, 34, 39, 51, 55, 59, 64, 65, 69, 78, 87, 92

Jesus Christ, 13, 22, 38, 65, 71, 90–1, 93
Judaism/Jews, 10, 13, 18, 21, 34, 37, 51, 53, 59, 62, 70, 72, 78, 80, 85, 87, 90

kachha, 36
kanga, 36
kara, 36
karma, 89
Kaur, 20
kesh, 36
ketubah, 62
Khalsa, 36
khitan, 23
kibbutz system, 70
Kiddush, 21, 37
kirpan, 20, 36
Krishna, 58

laws, 34, 50, 53, 65, 76, 80

mandaps, 60
Marduk, *9*
marriage/weddings, 22, 34, 45, 47, 51, 53, 55–67, 75
   arranged, 55, 60, 61, 64
   civil, 59
Matrimonial and Family Proceedings Act, 65
Mecca, 39, 92
menstruation/periods, 25, 43, 47, 48, 49
mohel, 21
moksha, 89
Mool Mantra, 20
moral codes/guidance, 13, 51, 71, 72
Moses, 37
Muhammad, 39, 92
mukti, 89
mummies, 88
mundan, 19

95

Nanak, Guru, 13
Neanderthal Man, 88
Nirvana, 89

Olam Ha'ba, 90
old age/the elderly, 69, 74–82, 84
old age pensions, 51, 56, 69, 74, 76–7
old people's homes, 79
Osiris, 88
out-of-the-body experiences, 92

Paradise, 92
parshad, 20, 36, 61
patriarchy, 42–3
Pentecost, 38
pillars of faith, five, 39
prasadam, 19
pregnancy, 32, 43–4, 49–50, 65, 68; *see also* abortion; conception; contraception; foetus, development of the; sex/the sexes
Purgatory, 91

Qur'an, the, 13, 59, 64, 69, 78, 92

Radha, 58
Ramadan, 39
Rastafarianism, 72
register/registry offices, 59
regression, 93
reincarnation, 19, 89; *see also* regression
resurrection, 90–2, 93
rites of initiation, 34–9
rites of passage, 12, 18–23, 34–9, 60–4; *see also* death
romalla, 20

Sabbath, 37, 62
sacraments, 59, 65
Sacred Thread ceremony, 34, 35
St Paul, 53, 65
salat prayers, 39
samskaras, 19
science/scientists, 7–8, 9, 10, 88, 91, 93
sex/the sexes, 26, 28, 31, 32, 34, 41–54, 75, 83
sexually transmitted diseases (STD), 48
sheltered accommodation, 79
Sheol, 90

shiva, 85
Sikhism/Sikhs, 13, 18, 20, 34, 36, 51, 55, 61, 69, 78, 87, 89
Singh, 20
smoking, 13, 31, 32, 34, 47
soul, the, 16, 17, 88–9, 90, 92
synagogues, 21, 37, 78

Tahneek, 18, 23
tefillin, 37
Ten Commandments, 13, 51, 72
Third World, the, 83–4
Tiamat, *9*
Torah, 37
Turin Shroud, 93

universe, the, 7–8, 9, 10, 17–18, 88
Upanayana, 35

Voluntary Euthanasia Society, 79–80

wuzu, 87